THE ANATOMY OF A LAWSUIT

CONTEMPORARY LEGAL EDUCATION SERIES

THE ANATOMY OF A LAWSUIT

Revised Edition

PETER N. SIMON
Professor of Law
University of Colorado

MICHIE
Law Publishers
CHARLOTTESVILLE, VIRGINIA

1310011

This book is dedicated to my dear wife, Kimberly Craven Simon, and to the memory of Joseph and Betty Simon and Lois Ann Craven

Preface to Revised Edition

This book is designed for two groups — beginning law students, and all others who have an interest in learning to understand the development of a lawsuit.

From the very beginning of law school, students are asked to read, understand, and even explain appellate opinions. After a while they will understand the context that produces these opinions, but at the beginning they must operate in a vacuum. In their courses they will have opinions ruling on the grant or denial of demurrers, summary judgments, directed verdicts, and the like, but they will have no real understanding, no "picture," of these important motions. This book is designed to give them an understanding of these motions. More importantly, it is designed to give them a feel for the development of an actual lawsuit — so that they can realize what it is that actually happens in the step-by-step development of a case. We have used the materials in this book for many years in the University of Colorado Law School orientation program, where they have served these purposes well. The initial edition of this work has also been used extensively at numerous other law schools throughout the country, assisting in the introduction of the real world of a lawsuit to thousands of budding new attorneys.

The book should also be suitable for use with undergraduate students and with all nonlawyers who would like to have a clearer picture of the workings of the legal system. I have tried to provide not only an introduction to the procedures used in a civil action, but also a broader perspective of the role that litigation plays in our society, so that the book can offer an interested layperson a serious introduction to a lawsuit.

This book is based on an actual case. Both attorneys (and their clients) were generous in sharing with me the details of the case. I have changed some of the documents for pedagogical purposes, but material from the trial transcripts is virtually verbatim — the voices are those of the real participants. In part to protect the privacy of the parties, and in part because the changes I have made make my account of the case significantly fictional, I have changed the names of the parties and the attorneys; I have also changed the dates. From my first contact with this case, I have been impressed with the manner in which the personalities shine through the "cold" transcript. The parties' words convey, much better than I could, just how much lawsuits turn upon the personalities and character of the participants.

The past few years have seen major changes in the rules governing pretrial development of the case. This edition reflects those changes. Plaintiff and Defendant exchange Disclosure Statements, negotiate a Discovery Plan and Scheduling Order, attend a Rule 26(f) Meeting and in general conduct discovery and pretrial negotiations all in accordance with the 1991 and 1993 amendments to the Federal Rules of Civil Procedure. In addition, the facts of the case have been updated, and where appropriate other changes have been made to make this book as current as this morning's newspaper. Of course, changing events over the next few years may require still further revision, but as of February 1996, this book is an accurate rendition of current litigation practice in the great majority of state and federal courts.

Peter N. Simon

February 1996 Boulder, Colorado

Table of Contents

TABLE OF CONTENTS

THE ANATOMY OF A LAWSUIT

A. INTRODUCTION

This book is the story of *Rasmussen v. Graham*, a lawsuit between two friends. The lawsuit resulted from an automobile accident that occurred while one was driving and the other was a passenger. Although their case went all the way to the Colorado Supreme Court, it was in most other regards a fairly typical lawsuit.

This book will trace their lawsuit from the accident through the pretrial procedures, the trial, and the appellate courts. It will use their case to demonstrate and explain each of the steps involved in the preparation and trial of a civil lawsuit in an American court; close attention will be paid to the procedural steps used under the recently revised rules of procedure used in the federal and most state court systems. Over and above procedures and rules, this case shows the effect individuals have on a lawsuit, and the effect that the lawsuit ultimately has on the litigants.

B. PREPARATION FOR TRIAL: PRETRIAL EVENTS AND ACTIONS

1. THE ACCIDENT

The two friends in this case were Anne Rasmussen and Paula Graham. At the time of the accident, they were both 17 years old, and were in their senior year at Fort Collins High School. They had been close friends for more than two years. The accident occurred during the course of a skiing vacation. Paula's father, Dr. Arthur Graham, owned a house trailer at Steamboat Springs. In early December, Paula, with her parents' permission, invited Anne to spend some time at the trailer at the end of the month. Anne agreed.

On Friday, December 26, Dr. and Mrs. Graham drove from Fort Collins to Steamboat Springs (about a four-hour drive), taking Anne's ski equipment with them. On Sunday, December 28, Paula and Anne drove from Fort Collins to Steamboat Springs in a 1987 blue Toyota Tercel that Dr. Graham had bought for Paula's use a few months earlier. Although it was thought of as Paula's car, the title was in Dr. Graham's name. Paula and Anne spent Sunday and Monday nights at the trailer, along with the Grahams and some guests of the Grahams. During that time the trailer's furnace broke down. Dr. Graham was able to keep the trailer heated, despite the very cold (-35°F) weather, by running two electric heaters and the kitchen oven, but the trailer's fuses kept blowing. Dr. Graham told Paula and Anne that, because of the heating problem, he did not want them staying in the trailer alone after he and Mrs. Graham returned to Fort Collins.

He arranged for them to stay with some friends in Steamboat Springs. Apparently they were not excited by the prospect. On the morning of Tuesday, December 30, Paula and Anne took Dr. Graham's key to the trailer and, without telling him, tried to have a duplicate made. They first tried the hardware store in Steamboat Springs, but that store did not have the proper blank from which to make the key. Then they drove to Craig, a town some 42 miles west of Steamboat Springs. There they were successful. After having the key made, they started back to Steamboat Springs.

Paula was driving, and she was in somewhat of a hurry. She was anxious to get home before lunch so that their absence would not be noted. At a point 15 miles west of Steamboat Springs, as they came over the crest of a slight hill, a large (12 ton) yellow road-maintainer with a snowplow came into view. It was four-tenths of a mile from them at the point it first became visible. It was in their lane (eastbound), but was travelling at only 4 miles per hour. Paula first pulled into the left (westbound) lane, hoping to pass the machine. An oncoming (westbound) pickup truck made that impossible. At that point she started to apply the brakes. The road was covered with snowpack, however, and the Tercel was unable to stop before hitting the road-maintainer.

Paula suffered a broken arm in the collision. Anne, who was sitting in the right front seat, hit her face on the dash. She suffered facial injuries, which were very painful and required extensive surgery and a fair degree of time to heal. She has not yet entirely recovered from the accident, and in some respects probably never will.

2. SETTLEMENT NEGOTIATIONS

Once her medical situation seemed fairly well stabilized, Anne and her parents began thinking about the possibility of obtaining some compensation from the Grahams' insurer, the Safeco Insurance Company. To help them negotiate, they contacted a Fort Collins attorney, William S. Hart. Hart was an experienced litigator. In fact, for a while he had served as the County Attorney for Larimer County.

Hart discussed the case at some length with Anne and her parents, outlining for them what he saw as the strong points and weak points of the case. In his view, a jury was likely to find that Paula had been negligent, that Anne was a sympathetic plaintiff, and that her injuries were substantial. The major obstacle in the case was the Colorado Guest Statute, which provided that in certain cases guests could not recover for the negligence of their hosts. Hart believed that the statute would not be applied in this case, but he also knew that there was a significant risk that a court would reach a different conclusion.

Hart also discussed the expenses of litigation. This was not an overly complicated case, so preparation would not be hugely expensive. But even if Hart made an effort to keep the costs down by limiting the use of expert testimony and formal discovery, the out of pocket expenses for preparing and trying the case were likely to be about $5,000, exclusive of Hart's fees. If Hart were to bill at his usual hourly rate ($125/hour), his time on the case would probably cost about $25,000.

Hart's hourly rate was not excessive. Hart worked about 40 to 45 hours a week. Of this time, however, only about 30 hours could be considered "billable." The rest was devoted to such matters as administering the office, professional reading, attending professional meetings and *pro bono* (charitable) representation of indigent clients. Thus, Hart had about 1,500 hours per year (30 hours times 50 weeks) for billable work. But this amount had to be reduced by a certain amount to reflect reduced bills where matters took longer than expected, or where the client had difficulty paying the full amount, or where Hart felt that the outcome did not justify charging the client the full amount. So, on an hourly rate, Hart's 1,500 hours were likely to generate about $150,000 in gross income for his office. This amount, however, had to pay for the substantial costs of operating an office, including rent, utilities, office equipment, salary and benefits for Hart's full-time secretary, professional malpractice and disability insurance, the expenses of maintaining a small library and on-line computer research, and membership in professional societies, all of which totalled about $90,000. So, at an hourly rate of $125, Hart would expect to average about $60,000 per year, not excessive in view of his experience, skills and success as a litigator.

Even though $25,000 would be a reasonable fee for representation in this action (by large city standards, it would be a bargain), it was still beyond the reach of the Rasmussens, as it would be with most families. Thus, if representation were available only on an hourly basis, Anne would not have been able to sue.

Hart believed that if Anne prevailed, she would recover in excess of $100,000. Of course, even in his view there was a significant chance that she would lose on the guest statute issue, and recover nothing — perhaps a one out of three possibility. If Anne won, she could surely afford to pay the costs of representation out of the proceeds of the case. But if she lost, she would not have the money to pay Hart.

In America, this conundrum is solved by the use of contingency fee arrangements — criticized heavily by institutional defendants but strongly believed in by a large segment of the profession. It is permissible in this country (but not in most others) for an attorney to be compensated by a fixed percentage of the proceeds. A typical arrangement, and the one used in this case, is for the attorney and the potential plaintiff to agree that the attorney will receive one-third of the gross amount paid by the defendant. If Anne were to lose the case, Hart would receive nothing, though professional rules require that she, and not Hart, remain responsible for the out of pocket expenses.[1] Hart and the Rasmussens executed a contingency fee agreement, and Hart began his representation of Anne.

Before leaving this topic, you should consider the arguments for and against permitting contingency fee arrangements. Critics believe that it encourages lawyers to encourage injured persons to sue, so that attorneys can generate large commissions on the lawsuits. They also argue that a lawyer who will receive one-third of any recovery is not likely to maintain professional objectivity and detachment; rather, she is likely to become so partisan that she will be more like a client than an attorney.

The economics of the arrangement can also pit the attorney *against* her client. Under a contingency fee agreement, an attorney is better off if the client accepts a quick settlement at the outset of a case, even if the settlement is for much less than the case is worth. For example, if Safeco had settled for $40,000, Hart would have received $13,300 for less than 10 hours work. If there is no settlement, Hart runs a very real risk of receiving no compensation; even if the outcome is very favorable, working up the case and trying it will use about 200 hours of Hart's time. So, about the best he could hope for would be a fee of $67,000 (one-third of $200,000), for 200 hours work. Obviously, a sure fee of $13,300 for 10 hours work (paid immediately) is a better deal for the attorney than a possible fee of $67,000 for 200 hours (paid, if at all, two years from now). The inducement for quick settlement is even stronger with less accomplished attorneys, who are somewhat scared of the courtroom, and know that even with a good case they stand a real possibility of losing if they don't accept the settlement. (To Hart's credit, he urged the Rasmussens to insist on more than $40,000, and when Safeco rejected their offer, he did not suggest that the Rasmussens lower their demand.)

The strongest argument in favor of the contingency fee is that it makes it possible for poor and middle class persons to sue when they have been injured. As this case demonstrates, most personal injury plaintiffs cannot afford representation unless their attorneys can be paid out of the proceeds, and an attorney will not agree to a substantial risk of non-payment unless the rewards for victory are proportionally increased. The pressure to settle quickly which is created by the contingency fee arrangement is not significantly worse than the conflict created by the usual hourly fee arrangement — which encourages

---

[1] This is so the attorney not be seen as financing the case — which, it is thought, would make the case look too much like a business venture and not enough like a professional arrangement. It is permissible, however, for the attorney to advance these expenses, and defer reimbursement until the end of the trial. As a practical matter, many attorneys will not insist on repayment of these amounts if plaintiff recovers nothing in the lawsuit.

attorneys to prolong litigation, even when their clients' interests might be better served by a quick settlement.

Hart's first task was to explore settlement possibilities with the opposing attorney. But before he commenced negotiations, Hart had to have a clear idea of the merits of Anne's case. While he did not expect a detailed legal discussion with Safeco's attorney, he needed to evaluate, realistically, what Anne would recover if they went to trial. If he was too optimistic, he might turn down a good offer, and then not do well at trial; if he was too pessimistic, he might accept a stingy offer, while holding out for more would have brought a better offer or a better result by going to trial. Furthermore, part of his job as Anne's negotiator would be to convince Safeco's attorney that Anne was so likely to win at trial that it was in Safeco's interest to offer a settlement; he could only do this if he had adequately researched Anne's case.

After a few meetings with the Rasmussens, Hart contacted Safeco, who in turn directed Hart to their attorney, Alfred Wilton. Hart and Wilton had both practiced in Fort Collins for a number of years, so they knew and respected each other. They could negotiate with little posturing or bravado.

Hart felt that Anne's case was very strong. He recommended that the Rasmussens set $60,000 as their bottom figure. (Their opening offer, of course, would be somewhat higher.) The Rasmussens disagreed. They were anxious to avoid litigation, so they instructed Hart that they were willing to settle for $40,000, and Hart ultimately passed that figure on to Wilton.

Wilton thought that Anne's case was not strong. The Colorado Guest Statute provided that in certain cases guests could not recover for the negligence of their hosts; Wilton believed this statute would provide a complete defense on the facts of this case. Based on Wilton's advice, Safeco's highest offer was $5,000, which they were clearly obligated to pay in any event, under the Medical Payments provision of the insurance policy.[2] The Grahams felt very badly about Anne's injuries, and were also anxious to avoid litigation. Dr. Graham offered to pay $10,000 of his own funds if Safeco would contribute the remaining $30,000 necessary to meet the Rasmussen figure. Safeco still refused to offer more than $5,000.

Safeco had a significant reason for taking such a strong position. As an insurance company, Safeco's business was defending lawsuits. They could estimate that defending this lawsuit might well cost them $30,000, even if they had a complete victory at trial (as they expected they would), so considering this lawsuit in isolation, they knew it would probably be less expensive to pay the

---

[2] In addition to the usual liability provisions, the Grahams' policy provided for the payment of the medical costs of the driver and any passenger in the Tercel, up to $5,000 per person, without regard to whose carelessness caused the accident. (Certain aspects of no-fault insurance applicable to this case have been modified, to simplify the book's discussion of the litigation issues.)

money to the plaintiff than to pay the costs of defending the lawsuit. But if plaintiffs knew that Safeco was willing to pay them the cost of defending a lawsuit even if Safeco expected to win at trial, plaintiffs with very weak cases would sue in the hope that Safeco would settle instead of defending. As an institutional defendant, it was very important that Safeco not take any steps that would encourage plaintiffs with weak lawsuits to sue. So Safeco and many other insurance companies have taken a general position against paying to settle cases which they expect to win at trial.

Hart and Wilton discussed their conflicting views of the case. Despite their mutual respect for each other, and despite their best efforts (over a period of time they had a number of discussions about settlement), they were too far apart to get the case settled. If Anne wanted compensation, she would have to sue.

Anne's theory of recovery was straightforward. If Anne could prove that Paula had been negligent in her operation of the automobile, and that that negligence had caused Anne's injuries, Anne would be entitled to an award of a sum of money, payable to her by Paula, sufficient (in theory) to compensate her for those injuries. This award would include compensation for the following items: first, her out-of-pocket expenses, such as doctor and hospital bills; second, the amount of income she lost and would continue to lose as a result of the injuries; third, the value of the impairment of her physical abilities; fourth, the loss in value of any personal possessions that might have been damaged by the accident; and finally, an amount calculated to be equal to the amount of "pain and suffering" caused her by the accident, both prior to the trial and in the future.

In all probability, Paula would not have enough money of her own to be able to pay Anne very much. A judgment against Paula, by itself, would not be worth much. However, Dr. Graham's insurance policy provided that, in the event of a lawsuit against one of the persons insured by the policy, Safeco would provide the defendant with an attorney, would pay all the costs of the defense, and would pay the amount of an award against the defendant up to $100,000. The persons insured by the policy included Paula.

The lawsuit would have a sort of hybrid quality. In almost all respects it was a suit against Paula. Hart would have to establish Paula's negligence and all the other elements necessary to support a recovery from Paula. If Hart should win the suit, however, Paula would not pay the judgment. Safeco would pay the judgment up to the $100,000 limit. Also, although Paula would be the named defendant, Safeco would choose and pay for her attorney in the case. In most ways, Safeco was the real defendant, but that fact would be concealed from the jury. If Hart so much as mentioned Safeco's interest in front of the jury, it might be enough to cause a mistrial.

QUESTION

Why might the mentioning of Safeco's interest in front of the jury cause a mistrial?

3. SELECTING THE PROPER COURT

Having exhausted the possibility of amicable settlement, Hart's next move was to commence the lawsuit. Before commencing the lawsuit, Hart had to choose the proper court in which the litigation should proceed. There are generally three aspects to this decision: subject matter jurisdiction, personal jurisdiction, and venue.

a. Subject Matter Jurisdiction

Subject matter jurisdiction refers to a court's authority to hear particular types of lawsuits. For example, many states have established specialized courts, which may handle only criminal matters, or divorces, or tax claims. Thus, if a court has special courts for probate, a person who tried to enforce a will in a general court would have her case dismissed for lack of subject matter jurisdiction. Most states have courts whose subject matter jurisdiction is limited to smaller disputes. For example, Colorado county courts only decide cases in which the amount in dispute is $5,000 or less. A person who commenced an action seeking enforcement of a $6,000 promissory note would have her case dismissed for lack of subject matter jurisdiction, unless she limited the amount she was seeking to the statutory maximum for the court.

There is one other aspect of subject matter jurisdiction which is of major importance. In addition to the court systems established by each of the 50 states, there is a system of courts established by Congress and acting under the authority of the federal government. As with state courts, the federal system is comprised of generalized courts, called United States District Courts, and specialized courts, such as the United States Tax Court and the Court of Claims.

There are United States District Courts in every state. For example, in Denver, one can find the United States District Court for the District of Colorado, and a few blocks away, the Colorado State District Court for Denver County. The personnel in one court are employees and officers of the United States; the personnel in the other are employees and officers of the State of Colorado and the City and County of Denver.

Some cases may only be tried in the federal court. Some may only be tried in the state court. Some may be tried in either. Some examples of cases which can only be tried in the federal court are most cases against the United States, cases in which a defendant is prosecuted for violation of a federal statute, cases involving collection of United States income, estate and gift taxes, and cases granting or revoking United States citizenship.

There are also cases which can be tried in state or federal courts, at the parties' option. Some examples include cases seeking civil damages for violation of a person's civil rights and cases between citizens of one state and citizens of another if more than $50,000 is in dispute.

While the existence of two separate systems of courts within the state can be confusing, there is one general rule to remember: the United States courts can only hear those cases which Congress has specifically given to them; if there is no statute providing for federal court jurisdiction over a type of case, then the federal courts may not hear that case. In this sense, all federal courts are considered to be courts of limited subject matter jurisdiction, and the first job of every litigant in federal court is to demonstrate that there is a federal statute specifically providing that this case can be tried in federal court.

With state courts, the opposite rule applies. The state trial court of general jurisdiction (e.g., the Colorado District Court) can hear any case between parties of any citizenship involving any subject matter, unless there is a statute or case law principle prohibiting it from hearing that type of case.

In our case, Anne was not basing her recovery on federal law, and the parties were not citizens of different states. The federal courts accordingly did not have subject matter jurisdiction of the dispute. There was no specialized state court for this sort of dispute, so the state court of general subject matter jurisdiction, the Colorado District Court, had subject matter jurisdiction over this case.

b. Personal Jurisdiction

If two New York citizens agreed to sue each other in a Colorado state court, that would be entirely permissible. But suppose the New York defendant did not wish to be sued in Colorado. It might be grossly unfair to require the New Yorker to travel all the way to Colorado, unless there were some particular connection between the New Yorker and Colorado. A long line of cases hold that the United States Constitution prohibits Colorado from asserting jurisdiction over citizens of other states who have little or no contact with Colorado. One would say that Colorado courts lack personal jurisdiction over non-Coloradans who have insufficient contacts with Colorado. Of course, Paula was a Colorado citizen, and she had substantial contacts with Colorado; Colorado courts could assert personal jurisdiction over her on either basis (citizenship or contacts).

c. Venue

Hart could and would sue Paula in a Colorado District Court. But there are twenty separate district courts within Colorado, located throughout the state. Just as the law of personal jurisdiction accomplishes a geographical allocation of judicial business among the fifty state court systems, the rules of venue effect a geographical distribution of judicial business among the various courts throughout the state.

Venue rules usually are embodied in a statute or court rule. Colorado provides for venue in the county where any defendant resides, or where the accident occurred, or (under certain circumstances) where any plaintiff resides. By these provisions, Hart could choose between bringing the action in Fort Collins (Larimer County), where Paula and Anne lived, or in Routt County, where the accident occurred. He chose the Colorado District Court in Larimer County.

QUESTION

What considerations are likely to have influenced Hart's decision to try the case in Larimer County, a suburban area, rather than Routt County, a more rural, mountainous area?

4. COMMENCEMENT OF THE ACTION: COMPLAINT, SUMMONS, AND SERVICE OF PROCESS

To initiate the litigation, Hart has to draft a document called a "complaint." (In other states Hart's initial pleading might be called a "petition," a "statement of claim," or a "declaration.") The action will be formally commenced when Hart files the complaint with the clerk of the Larimer County District Court. After commencing the lawsuit, Hart has to arrange for copies of the complaint and a summons to be "served upon" each defendant. It is this service that brings the defendant into the lawsuit, and makes her a party subject to the court's jurisdiction and to all of the court's rulings. Until she is served, she is not a party in the lawsuit and is not subject to the court's rulings.

a. The Complaint

What must Hart put in the complaint? To answer this question we must give some thought to what functions the complaint (and indeed the whole process of pleading) is designed to serve. Views of this have changed a good deal over the years. Centuries ago, under the English common-law pleading system (from which our present procedure has evolved), the pleadings were expected to define the dispute between the parties with great precision. This proved an illusory goal. The rules governing pleading became increasingly technical and complex. Meritorious claims were lost because of minor errors in the way pleadings were drafted. In England, by the beginning of the nineteenth century, the outcome of a case seemed as likely to turn on the skill of the pleaders as on the merits of the parties' respective positions. The situation was intolerable, and reforms enacted by Parliament in 1833 and 1873 succeeded in solving most of the worst problems. (The writings of Charles Dickens and Jeremy Bentham, which were highly critical of the system, made a huge contribution to the mood that led to these reforms.)

The situation in this country, though never quite as bad as that in England, was still quite formalistic. In 1848, New York adopted a Code of Civil Procedure, largely drafted by David Dudley Field. During the next few decades, most of the states (excepting those on the eastern seaboard) adopted the Field Code.

The Code was a substantial improvement over the common-law system of procedure, and it succeeded in simplifying a number of unnecessary complexities in trial court practice. This was especially true in the practice of pleading. The Code required that the complaint contain a "plain and concise statement of the facts constituting plaintiff's cause of action." Unfortunately, the Code still used the pleadings as a means of narrowing and defining the dispute. This, coupled with a generally unsympathetic reception by a judiciary accustomed to the hypertechnicalities of common-law pleading, led to the result that pleading under the Code also became quite complex and technical — though certainly not nearly as bad as what had preceded it.

By adopting the Field Code, state legislatures had assumed the responsibility of creating a system of procedure. While this was a marked improvement over the ad hoc, step-by-step development of the common-law system, the legislative process proved too cumbersome. In the English Judiciary Reform Act of 1873, Parliament authorized the English courts to promulgate a system of rules. In America, after a long campaign, Congress in 1936 authorized the Supreme Court to promulgate rules for use in the federal courts. The Supreme Court appointed a committee to draft such rules. Under the leadership of Charles E. Clark, Dean of the Yale Law School and a leading scholar on Code pleading, the committee drafted the Federal Rules of Civil Procedure. These took effect in federal courts in 1938, and they have proven to be quite effective. Because of the rulemaking authority that was delegated (with certain qualifications) to the Supreme Court, it has been much easier for unsuccessful portions of the Federal Rules to be amended. Indeed, the Federal Rules have proven so successful in the federal courts that a majority of the states have adopted them for use in their own courts; even in the states that have not done so, procedural developments have been heavily influenced by the Federal Rules.

In contrast to the Code, the Federal Rules rejected the use of the pleadings as a means of narrowing or defining the dispute. The complaint's main function now is to identify the transaction which led to plaintiff's lawsuit. Fed. R. Civ. P. 8(a) provides that the complaint "shall contain ... (2) a short and plain statement of the claim showing that the pleader is entitled to relief, and (3) a demand for judgment for the relief to which he deems himself entitled." Anticipating that this formula could easily be misinterpreted in the same as the Code's "plain and concise statement of the facts," the drafters of the Federal Rules used a device that had proven very successful in England in 1875, and later in Connecticut. A series of sample pleadings were included as part of the rules. Fed. R. Civ. P. 84 (as amended) provided that these sample pleadings were to be considered sufficient. The simplicity of these sample pleadings left little room for the development of hypertechnical pleading requirements.

Recent amendments to the Federal Rules have created some incentives to use more complete pleadings. In 1993 the Federal Rules were amended to require that participants exchange substantial disclosures of documents, witness lists, and other information shortly after the case begins. But these disclosure requirements only apply to "facts alleged with particularity in the pleadings." Under these rules, a party whose pleadings are too simple will not obtain important information from the other party. So it appears that the pendulum is beginning to swing back towards more detailed pleadings. It remains to be seen whether these new requirements will lead to protracted disputes over how "particular" allegations must be to trigger the disclosure requirement.

Colorado adopted the Federal Rules for Colorado state courts shortly after they became effective in the federal courts. Colorado's rules include the following as an example of the simplicity permissible in a negligence action complaint:

> 1. On June 1, 1939, in a public highway called Broadway Street in Denver, Colorado, defendant negligently drove a motor vehicle against plaintiff who was then crossing said highway.
>
> 2. As a result plaintiff was thrown down and had his leg broken and was otherwise injured, was prevented from transacting his business, suffered great pain of body and mind, and incurred expenses for medical attention and hospitalization in the sum of .... dollars.
>
> Wherefore plaintiff demands judgment against defendant in the sum of .... dollars and costs.

While Hart could have filed a similarly simple complaint, he chose instead to file the following:[3]

---

[3] A number of changes have been made in the complaint, and in each of the other documents set out below. Copies of the original pleadings are on file in the Clerk's Office, Larimer County District Court, Fort Collins, Colorado (Civil Action No. 20395), and in the Clerk's Office, Colorado Court of Appeals, Denver, Colorado (Appeal No. 71477).

IN THE DISTRICT COURT

IN AND FOR THE COUNTY OF LARIMER

AND STATE OF COLORADO

Division I

Civil Action No. 20395

ANNE RASMUSSEN,	)	
	)	
Plaintiff,	)	
	)	
vs.	)	COMPLAINT
	)	
PAULA GRAHAM and ROGER GRAHAM,	)	
	)	
Defendants.	)	

FIRST CLAIM

The plaintiff Anne Rasmussen, by her attorney, William S. Hart, for her FIRST CLAIM FOR RELIEF, alleges:

1. That on or about December 30, 1993, at a point on United States Highway No. 40 approximately 15 miles West of Steamboat Springs, Colorado, in the County of Routt and State of Colorado, the defendant Paula Graham did so negligently and carelessly operate a motor vehicle in which the plaintiff Anne Rasmussen was a passenger that said motor vehicle struck a snowplow and caused severe injuries to said plaintiff.

2. That as a direct and proximate result of the negligence and carelessness of the defendants, plaintiff Anne Rasmussen sustained numerous and severe permanent and disabling injuries including, but not limited to, lacerations, contusions, and fractures of the bones of the head, face, and jaw, and as a direct and proximate result thereof, plaintiff Anne Rasmussen will be permanently disabled and disfigured for the rest of her natural life.

3. That as a direct and proximate result of the negligence and carelessness of the defendants as aforesaid, plaintiff has incurred reasonable and necessary hospital, medical and drug expenses to the date of filing the Complaint herein, as follows:

Routt County Hospital, Steamboat Springs, Colo.	$ 551.00
Presbyterian Medical Center	5,410.70
Dec. 30, 1993 to January 12, 1994	
Presbyterian Medical Center	2,404.70
Feb. 12, 13, 14, 1993	
Routt County Ambulance Service	107.00
Dr. C. K. Mammel, Denver, Colo.	877.00

Dr. William O. Smith, Denver, Colo.	135.00
Dr. B. Ackles, Denver, Colo.	165.00
Dr. I. Cregger, Denver, Colo.	107.00
Dr. Vernon Price, Steamboat Springs, Colo.	125.00
Dr. William Scoutland, Denver, Colo.	150.00
Dr. James Hoffman, Ft. Collins, Colo.	115.00
Dr. Thomas Bennett, Ft. Collins, Colo.	112.00
Radiologist	26.00
Drugs	336.00
Total	$10,621.40

to her total damage in the sum of Ten Thousand Six Hundred Twenty-One Dollars and Forty Cents ($10,621.40).

4. That as a direct and proximate result of the negligence and carelessness of the defendants as aforesaid, the plaintiff's clothing was permanently destroyed, to her damage of One Hundred Fifty Dollars ($150.00).

5. That as a direct and proximate result of the negligence and carelessness of the defendants as aforesaid, plaintiff has sustained certain permanent injuries that will prevent her from receiving a music scholarship at Colorado State University, to her damage in the sum of Eight Thousand Dollars ($8,000.00).

6. That as a direct and proximate result of the negligence and carelessness of the defendants as aforesaid, the plaintiff will incur medical and drug expenses throughout the rest of her natural life because of the permanence of her said injuries, all to her damage in the estimated sum of Twenty-Five Thousand Dollars ($25,000.00).

7. That as a direct and proximate result of the negligence and carelessness of the defendants as aforesaid, the plaintiff Anne Rasmussen has sustained great physical pain and suffering and will continue to have pain and suffering in the future all to her damage in the sum of Fifty Thousand Dollars ($50,000.00).

8. That as a direct and proximate result of the negligence and carelessness of the defendants aforesaid, the plaintiff Anne Rasmussen has sustained a substantial facial disfigurement that has caused her great emotional and mental pain and suffering and will continue to cause her emotional and mental pain and suffering in the future, all to her damage in the sum of Fifty Thousand Dollars ($50,000.00).

9. That as a direct and proximate result of the negligence and carelessness of the defendants aforesaid, the plaintiff Anne Rasmussen has sustained and suffered a permanent impairment of her ability to earn income throughout the rest of her natural life, all to her damage in the sum of Fifty Thousand Dollars ($50,000.00).

WHEREFORE, plaintiff Anne Rasmussen demands judgment against the defendant Paula Graham in the total sum of One Hundred Ninety-Three Thousand Seven Hundred Seventy-One Dollars and Forty Cents ($193,771.40) for her permanent, disabling, and disfiguring injuries, her pain and suffering, her medical and drug expenses and loss of future earnings that she has sustained

13

to date and will sustain for the rest of her natural life, together with her costs, interest from the date of filing the Complaint herein, and for such other and further relief as the Court deems proper.

SECOND CLAIM

Plaintiff Anne Rasmussen, by her attorney WILLIAM S. HART, for her SECOND CLAIM FOR RELIEF, hereby incorporates each and every allegation of her First Claim for Relief, and further alleges:

10. That the motor vehicle being driven by the defendant Paula Graham was owned, kept, and maintained by the defendant Roger Graham.

11. That the defendant Paula Graham was driving said automobile with the permission of the defendant Roger Graham.

WHEREFORE, plaintiff Anne Rasmussen demands judgment against the defendant Roger Graham in the total sum of One Hundred Ninety-Three Thousand Seven Hundred Seventy-One Dollars and Forty Cents ($193,771.40) for her permanent, disabling and disfiguring injuries, her pain and suffering, her medical and drug expenses and loss of future earnings that she has sustained to date and will sustain for the rest of her natural life, together with her costs, interest from the date of filing the Complaint herein, and for such other and further relief as the Court deems proper.

THIRD CLAIM

For her THIRD CLAIM FOR RELIEF, an alternative to her First Claim for Relief, plaintiff, by her attorney, hereby incorporates each and every allegation of her First Claim for Relief, and further alleges:

12. That the negligence of the defendant Paula Graham consisted of a willful and wanton disregard of the rights, safety and well-being of the plaintiff.

WHEREFORE, plaintiff Anne Rasmussen demands judgment against the defendant Paula Graham in the total sum of One Hundred Ninety-Three Thousand Seven Hundred Seventy-One Dollars and Forty Cents ($193,771.40) for her permanent, disabling and disfiguring injuries, her pain and suffering, her medical and drug expenses and loss of future earnings that she has sustained to date and will sustain for the rest of her natural life, together with her costs, interest from the date of filing the Complaint herein, and for such other and further relief as the Court deems proper.

FOURTH CLAIM

For her FOURTH CLAIM FOR RELIEF, an alternative to her Second Claim for Relief, plaintiff, by her attorney, hereby incorporates each and every allegation of her First Claim for Relief, of her Second Claim for Relief, and of her Third Claim for Relief.

WHEREFORE, plaintiff Anne Rasmussen demands judgment against the defendant Roger Graham in the total sum of One Hundred Ninety-Three Thousand Seven Hundred Seventy-One Dollars and Forty Cents ($193,771.40) for her permanent, disabling and disfiguring injuries, her pain and suffering, her medical and drug expenses and loss of future earnings that she has sustained to date and will sustain for the rest of her natural life, together with her costs, interest from the date of filing the Complaint herein, and for such other and further relief as the Court deems proper.

December 12, 1994

[Signed] William S. Hart
Attorney for Plaintiff
[Address and Telephone Omitted]

QUESTIONS

1. This complaint is a good bit more complex than Form 9. Under Rule 84, Hart would have been safe with a complaint as short as the form; if that is so, why do you suppose he drafted the complaint set out above? Does the added detail help his case? If so, how?

2. Note that the complaint is drawn in factual terms, though many of the "facts" (such as item 12) are little more than the statement of a desired legal conclusion. The ordering of the facts alleged, however, clearly reveals the legal theories on which Hart seeks to rely for recovery. Consider the Second Claim. Who is the target of that claim? Judging solely from the claim, what would you think Hart must show in order to prevail? Make a one-word or two-word label for each paragraph in the first and second claims for relief. These labels should show you how Hart hopes to develop his case. The third and fourth claims for relief add one additional factual allegation. As you will see, this factual allegation is added in anticipation of a defense Hart thinks likely to be raised by the defendant's attorney. Defer your full consideration of the third and fourth claims for relief until we discuss the guest statute defense (see pp. 24, *et seq.*, *infra*). Notice that Safeco does not appear in the complaint at all.

b. The Filing of the Complaint and the Issuance of the Summons *How ACTION the Begins*

Fed. R. Civ. P. 3 provides that "A civil action is commenced by filing a complaint with the court." Pursuant to this rule, Hart carried an original and three copies of the Complaint to the clerk's office in the Larimer County District Courthouse. There he handed the original and two of the copies to a deputy clerk, along with a filing fee. The action was then "commenced." The deputy clerk assigned a number to the case and then issued a summons for each defendant. A copy of the summons to Paula follows.

IN THE DISTRICT COURT

IN AND FOR THE COUNTY OF LARIMER

AND STATE OF COLORADO

Division I

Civil Action No. 20395

ANNE RASMUSSEN,	)	
	)	
Plaintiff,	)	
	)	
vs.	)	SUMMONS
	)	
PAULA GRAHAM and ROGER GRAHAM,	)	
	)	
Defendants.	)	

To the above named defendants:

You are hereby summoned and required to serve upon WILLIAM S. HART, plaintiff's attorney, whose address is [omitted], an answer to the complaint which is herewith served upon you, within 20 days after service of this summons upon you, exclusive of the day of service. If you fail to do so, judgment by default will be taken against you for the relief demanded in the complaint.

December 14, 1994   [Signed] Roger Finger
                                                                       Clerk of the Court

---

In some states each summons, with a copy of the complaint, would be sent to the office of the sheriff or some equivalent official. A deputy sheriff would then be assigned to "serve" the summons and the copy of the complaint on each defendant. In Colorado and in the federal courts, the summons may be served by any adult not otherwise associated with the suit. The traditional and still most common manner of service is for the person making service to hand copies of the summons and the complaint (together referred to as the "process") to the defendant in person. The server keeps the original summons in his possession. Needless to say, defendants are sometimes reluctant to accept the process, and the job of process server requires cleverness, guile, and the ability to withstand occasional physical abuse. Most states now provide that a defendant who refuses to accept process that is offered shall be treated as though the process has been accepted.

16

Once the process has been served, the process server must complete a "return of service." This return of service will state (in most states under oath) the manner in which the service was made. This statement will be written on either the lower portion or the reverse side of the original summons, which will then be returned to the clerk's office. The clerk's file will now show the complaint, whether or not each defendant was served, and if so, how.

Paula and Dr. Graham each were served. According to both the summons and the rules upon which it is based, each defendant then had twenty days to respond. The next step in the development of the lawsuit is up to them.

5. DEFENDANT'S RESPONSES: MOTIONS TO DISMISS, ANSWERS, AND COUNTERCLAIMS

At this point in the litigation, all that has happened is that Anne has commenced the action, and has made certain allegations and demands. As a general matter, four defensive responses and one offensive response are available to the defendants. The defensive responses are as follows:

1. The defendant can attack the manner in which the action was commenced by a motion to dismiss or a motion to quash service. In effect, such a motion says, "We need not respond because of a procedural error in the way the action was commenced." Some typical examples would be motions to dismiss based on improper service, lack of personal or subject matter jurisdiction, or lack of venue.

2. The defendant can take the position that even if the plaintiff's allegations are correct, she is not entitled to a recovery. In effect, this response says, "The law does not provide for damages for the facts you have alleged." This is accomplished by a motion to dismiss for failure to state a claim upon which relief can be granted, referred to in some jurisdictions as a general demurrer.

3. The defendant can deny the allegations of the complaint. In effect, this response says, "The evidence will show that your allegations not true." This is referred to as a negative defense to the merits and is raised by a pleading called an "answer."

4. The defendant can assert an affirmative defense, also in the answer. In effect, this response says, "Plaintiff omitted some information that exonerates me."

The defendant's offensive response is known as a counterclaim. As a functional matter, it is a close relative of the complaint. In the counterclaim, the defendant may seek the same types of relief (such as money damages) available to the plaintiff in the complaint. The counterclaim is available to the defendant in those situations where there would be a proper basis for filing a complaint against the person who is now the plaintiff if the plaintiff had not sued first. These responses are not exclusive, and defendants will frequently combine two or more of them.

The Grahams, of course, knew that Anne was about to commence a lawsuit. They had been involved in the negotiations between Hart and Wilton which took place prior to the commencement of the action. So, when the Grahams were served, Dr. Graham contacted Wilton, as he had been instructed to do, and gave him the documents which had been served upon him and upon Paula. Wilton then reviewed the facts of the case and decided which of above responses was worth pursuing.

a. Motion to Dismiss for a Procedural Defect in the Commencement of the Action

Fed. R. Civ. P. 12(b) specifies certain defects in the complaint that can be tested by motion.[4] If Wilton had found any of these defects, he could have sought dismissal by a simple motion. For example, suppose the process server, instead of actually handing the copies of the summons and complaint to Dr. Graham, had simply placed them on Dr. Graham's desk while Dr. Graham was sitting there. Most courts would probably consider that sufficient to constitute proper service, but Wilton would be entitled to a definitive answer. He could raise the question by the following motion.

IN THE DISTRICT COURT

IN AND FOR THE COUNTY OF LARIMER

AND STATE OF COLORADO

Division I

Civil Action No. 20395

ANNE RASMUSSEN,	)	
	)	
Plaintiff,	)	
	)	
vs.	)	MOTION TO QUASH
	)	SERVICE OF PROCESS
PAULA GRAHAM and ROGER GRAHAM,	)	
	)	
Defendants.	)	

---

[4]The defenses numbered (2) through (5) in Fed. R. Civ. P. 12(b) are the ones that involve procedural defects.

Defendant Roger Graham, through his attorney, hereby moves that the Court quash service of process upon him.

January 5, 1994   [Signed] Alfred Wilton
                                   Attorney for Defendants
                                   [Address and Telephone
                                   Omitted]

This motion would be accompanied by a memorandum in support of the motion, in which Wilton would present arguments and legal authorities showing why the service of process should be considered inadequate. The originals of the motions and the memorandum would be filed with the court, by mailing a copy to the clerk's office. Wilton would mail a copy of each of the documents to Hart. Hart would then have an opportunity to file a memorandum in opposition to the motion. Unless the attorneys waived oral arguments, both attorneys would appear before the judge at the time set for argument. Wilton, as the moving party, would first present his arguments. Hart could then respond. Wilton could then reply, and so on, until either the judge decided she had heard enough, or the attorneys had run out of things to say. The judge might rule from the bench, or take the matter under advisement, in which case she would rule on the motion after a few days or weeks.

As you can tell from the above description, a motion is simply a formal request by a party that the court make a particular ruling — in this case, a ruling that the process be quashed. The procedure followed with all motions would be substantially the same. The judge will either "deny" or "grant" the motion. In either case, the judge's decision will be made in a "ruling." Whichever way the judge rules, the losing party might claim later, on appeal, that the ruling was erroneous. Many of the appellate court opinions you will read will be addressing such contentions. It may be necessary for the judge to issue an "order" implementing the ruling on the motion. Here, if the judge were to grant Wilton's request, an order would be issued quashing service of process on defendant Roger Graham. Graham would then be in the position of a defendant who had been named in the Complaint, but had not been served. Plaintiff would be free to have process served upon Graham again, thereby bringing him into the lawsuit. If plaintiff did not do this, the action against Graham would ultimately be dismissed.

b. Motion to Dismiss for Failure to State a Claim Upon Which Relief Can Be Granted

Fed. R. Civ. P. 12(b)(6) provides for a motion to dismiss for failure to state a claim. In common-law pleading this motion was called a demurrer to the declaration, and in Code pleading a general demurrer. In effect, this motion asserts that even if all of the allegations of fact set forth in the complaint are established, plaintiff will not be entitled to a recovery. What this usually means is that the parties have a dispute as to the applicable legal rule. For the purpose of considering this motion, the court will temporarily assume that plaintiff will be able to prove each of the facts alleged in the complaint. For this reason, the motion (or the demurrer) is said to admit the allegations of the complaint. In common-law pleading, the party demurring was bound by this "admission." In modern practice, if the demurrer or motion is denied, the defendant is free to contest any or all of the allegations of the complaint, as if no demurrer or motion had been made.

This is an important device. You will find that many of the opinions you read will concern the question of whether a demurrer or motion to dismiss should have been granted by the trial court. We will take a close look at the Rule 12(b)(6) motion filed by Wilton in this case.

Wilton, after an examination of the complaint and some research, came to the conclusion that Claims 2 and 4, the claims against Dr. Graham, might well be subject to a Rule 12(b)(6) motion. The only allegations connecting Dr. Graham with the injuries were the allegations that Dr. Graham owned the car and that he gave permission to Paula to drive it. These allegations would be sufficient to support a judgment against Dr. Graham only if, under Colorado law, the owner of an automobile were responsible for injuries caused by the negligence of the driver of that automobile, where the driver had the owner's permission to operate the vehicle. If Colorado does not recognize such a theory, then Anne has not stated any basis for recovery against Roger Graham. The question, then, is one of substantive law (i.e., the law regulating the day-to-day conduct of people). It turns on the legal consequences of owning a car in Colorado, and not on the rules of pleading or procedure.

How was the question decided? The procedure followed was that used for any motion. Ultimately, the court decided which view of the substantive law was correct and an order was issued. How did the court rule? A number of states have adopted statutes providing that the owner of an automobile is liable for injuries to third persons caused by the negligence of any person who is operating the car with the owner's consent, but Colorado had no such statute. One state had adopted this rule by an opinion of its Supreme Court, but that state was Florida, not Colorado. Indeed, in a number of opinions, the Colorado Supreme Court had rejected this doctrine. At oral argument, Wilton stressed these opinions. Hart acknowledged that the weight of authority was against his position. He argued, however, that the logic of modern conditions was against these authorities, and that the trial judge should anticipate the Colorado Supreme Court's overruling those earlier precedents. His argument was based on the increasingly widespread use of insurance. The owner, not the user, of an automobile, he argued, is the person likely to be covered by automobile insurance, and, therefore, in order for the injured person to get the benefits of the insurance policy, he ought to be able to sue the owner (likely to be insured) as well as the driver (not as likely to be insured). The number of legislatures that recently had passed "owner consent statutes" showed that this was the modern trend.

Hart was asking Judge Shannon to substitute his opinion regarding social policy for the command of precedent. Occasionally judges will do this when the precedent is old or unclear and the social policy insistent — particularly if a claim can be made that the precedent is not applicable to this case for some reason (i.e., if it can be "distinguished" from this case). But in this case, the precedents were clear, recent, and indistinguishable, and the policy arguments were balanced. Hart must have know that Judge Shannon would grant Wilton's motion and dismiss the claims against Roger Graham. So why did he include those claims in his complaint?

Hart believed that the Colorado Supreme Court might be convinced to change its position. While a trial judge must defer to Supreme Court opinions, the Supreme Court is free to change its mind from time to time. But the Supreme Court will only consider an issue if it was raised in the trial court, so that the trial judge and the opposing party had a fair chance to deal with it before the end of the trial. Hart could only present the matter to the Supreme Court if he had first presented it to the trial court. Thus, even though he knew that Judge Shannon would deny the claims against Roger Graham, Hart included them in the complaint in order to preserve his right to present the issue to the Supreme Court.

To no one's surprise, Judge Shannon granted Wilton's motion to dismiss the claims against Roger Graham. The Judge's brief opinion stated: *Judge granted Graham's motion*

> The large number of legislatures which have adopted owner consent statutes, and the paucity of judicial adoption of the plaintiff's position, suggest that the Colorado Supreme Court would view this as a matter for the legislature. Even if that Court were willing to reconsider their earlier position, I think it unlikely that they would overrule the earlier cases. I base this conclusion on the widely known fact that virtually all automobile liability insurance policies now issued extend coverage to all persons driving with the owner's consent. For that reason, there is no real advantage to be had by extending liability to a person who is not alleged to have engaged in any culpable activity.
>
> Claims 2 and 4 of the complaint are hereby dismissed, with leave to file an amended complaint within 10 days.

The "leave" provided at the end of the opinion gave Hart permission to file an "amended complaint" including additional factual allegations that would support a recovery against Dr. Graham. For example, suppose Dr. Graham knew that

Paula was a very careless driver, but gave her the keys to the car anyway. Hart could amend the complaint to allege that fact, which would then predicate Graham's liability on his own negligent act.

In this case Hart could not amend the complaint to include allegations of personal culpability on Dr. Graham's part because there was no evidence to support such allegations. Under Rule 54(b), judgment in favor of Roger Graham will not actually be entered until the entire case is over. For practical purposes, however, the action against Roger is at an end, unless Hart ultimately appeals the trial judge's ruling.

c. The Answer: Negative Defenses

Under the Rules, the facts of the complaint are taken as true, unless they are denied in the answer. Thus, in drafting her answer, the defendant must carefully review the complaint, identify the facts which she is willing to concede (such as the fact that an accident occurred at the time and place alleged), and deny every factual allegation that she wants to dispute.

Factual allegations may be denied in two ways. If defendant believes the factual allegation to be untrue, she may simply state this. If she does not know whether or not the fact exists, she may state in her answer that "she is without knowledge or information sufficient to form a belief" as to that fact, which will be considered a sufficient denial of the factual allegation. But if she does not do one or the other, she will be treated as having admitted the factual allegation, and it will be incontrovertible for the rest of the case.

As you remember, the claims against Dr. Graham were dismissed on his 12(b)(6) motion. As to Paula, however, no motions were filed, and she was therefore required to file an answer within 20 days. An answer, like a motion, is filed by mailing the original to the clerk of the court and mailing a copy to the plaintiff's attorney.

Within the required period, Wilton filed the following answer:

IN THE DISTRICT COURT

IN AND FOR THE COUNTY OF LARIMER

AND STATE OF COLORADO

Division I

Civil Action No. 20395

ANNE RASMUSSEN,	)	
	)	
Plaintiff,	)	
	)	
vs.	)	ANSWER
	)	
PAULA GRAHAM and ROGER GRAHAM,	)	
	)	
Defendants.	)	

Defendant Paula Graham, by her attorney Alfred Wilton, answers plaintiff's complaint as follows:

FIRST DEFENSE (Denials of the Allegations of the Complaint)

As to the allegations of plaintiff's First Claim:

1. Defendant admits that an accident occurred between the motor vehicle being driven by defendant Paula Graham and a snowplow, at the time and place set out in Paragraph 1 of the complaint, and denies each and every other allegation of Paragraph 1 of the Complaint.

2. Defendant admits that Plaintiff was injured in said accident, but denies each and every allegation of Paragraph 2 of the Complaint.

3. Defendant lacks information and belief concerning the amount of Plaintiff's medical expenses, and denies each and every other allegation of Paragraph 3 of the complaint.

4. Defendant lacks information and belief concerning the value of Plaintiff's clothing, and denies each and every other allegation of Paragraph 4 of the Complaint.

5. Plaintiff lacks information and belief concerning Plaintiff's injuries and her alleged musical scholarship, and denies each and every other allegation of Paragraph 5 of the Complaint.

6. Plaintiff denies the allegations of Paragraph 6 of the Complaint.

7. Plaintiff denies the allegations of Paragraph 7 of the Complaint.

8. Plaintiff denies the allegations of Paragraph 8 of the Complaint.

9. Plaintiff denies the allegations of Paragraph 9 of the Complaint.

As to the allegations of the Second Claim: This claim has been dismissed by order of the Court.

As to the allegations of the Third Claim:

12. Plaintiff denies the allegations of Paragraph 12 of the Complaint.

As to the allegations of the Fourth Claim: This claim has been dismissed by order of the Court.

SECOND DEFENSE (Affirmative Defense: Colorado Guest Statute)

[Omitted for later discussion.]

January 5, 1994
                    [Signed] Alfred Wilton
                    Attorney for Defendant
                    [Address and Telephone Omitted]

QUESTIONS

1. What facts were placed in issue? Did Wilton deny any facts which he should have admitted? *Med Expenses, value of clothing, alleged scholarity* [handwritten]

2. Why would a defendant's attorney ever admit any of the complaint's allegations? (Consider Fed. R. Civ. P. 11.) Do the complaint and the answer seem an effective means of eliminating unnecessary factual issues from a dispute?

d. The Answer: Affirmative Defenses

Up to this point, the scope of the factual inquiry has been largely determined by the plaintiff. Defendant's motions to dismiss either ignored the factual allegations or assumed them to be true, and the negative defenses were responses only to the factual assertions of the plaintiff. On occasion, however, there are facts not alleged in the complaint which, if alleged and proved by defendant, will provide a defense for the defendant. Because the defendant must come forward first with the facts concerning this type of defense, it is called an "affirmative defense."

In the 1920's and 1930's, largely at the behest of insurance companies but also as a reflection of solicitude towards generous drivers, a number of states enacted legislation, commonly known as guest statutes, protecting automobile drivers and owners from lawsuits brought by guests who had been injured in their vehicles. Colorado's guest statute, adopted in 1931, provided the following:

> *Guest has no cause of action — when.* — No person transported by the owner or operator of a motor vehicle as his guest, without payment for such transportation, shall have a cause of action for damages against such owner or operator for injury, death or loss in case of accident, unless such accident shall have been intentional on the part of such owner or operator or caused

by his intoxication, or by negligence consisting of a willful and wanton disregard of the rights of others ....[5]

QUESTIONS

1. Does the guest statute take away Anne's lawsuit? Read it again carefully, and then list all the situations in which the statute permits an injured person to recover from the driver of the car which she was in when she was injured. Can Anne fit her case into any of these situations? What further information would you need to know?

2. At this point, you should re-examine the Complaint's third claim for relief. Is it now clear why Hart added this theory?

3. On the basis of what we have discussed to this point, both as to the facts of the case and the general information about lawsuits, you should be able to draft the allegations necessary to raise the affirmative defense created by the guest statute. Determine, from a careful reading of the language of the statute, the facts that Wilton will have to establish to prevail on this defense, and then draft a paragraph, making the necessary allegations. (Wilton's second defense, of course, was just such a paragraph.)

You will note that the paragraph you have just drafted alleges the existence of certain facts, in a fashion similar to that of the complaint. Unlike the allegations of the complaint, the allegations of the answer are considered denied unless they are specifically admitted.

Why not treat the allegations of the answer in the same fashion as facts alleged in the complaint (i.e., admitted unless specifically denied)? In older practice, every new fact alleged in the answer would have to be denied by the plaintiff in a pleading known as a *reply*. Then, if there were new facts alleged in the reply, the defendant would have to file a pleading denying those new allegations, and so on. The drafters of the Federal Rules decided that ordinarily one round of pleadings should be enough. The allegations of the answer are considered automatically denied, so that the plaintiff will not have to file an additional pleading to deny them.

e. The Answer: Counterclaims

The purpose of the defenses just discussed is to avoid liability on the defendant's part. There are some situations in which the defendant should be able to do more than avoid paying the plaintiff. Suppose, for example, the accident had occurred because Anne, in a fit of anger, had hit Paula, causing her to lose control of the car. If Anne had sued Paula under those circumstances, Paula

---

[5] Such statutes have become increasingly unpopular, and a number of states have repealed their guest statutes in recent years.

would certainly want to prove that fact as a defense to her liability, but she would also want to sue Anne, to recover damages for her (Paula's) broken arm and her broken Tercel.

The device Paula would use is called a counterclaim. It is very similar to a complaint, except for the fact that it is found as part of a defendant's answer. When a defendant includes a counterclaim in the answer, it is very much as though a separate action had been commenced against the plaintiff. Paula would allege the existence of certain facts (Anne's conduct, the accident it caused, and Paula's injuries), and include a paragraph demanding judgment against Anne for a certain sum of money.

While a plaintiff need not (indeed, may not) file a reply to the usual answer, she must file a reply to an answer which includes a counterclaim. This is because a counterclaim functions exactly as a complaint, and there is some importance in determining which allegations of the counterclaim will be disputed. Counterclaims are sometimes confused with affirmative defenses. But the significant difference is that an affirmative defense seeks to avoid a claim against the defendant, while a counterclaim seeks affirmative relief (such as damages or an injunction) against the plaintiff. It is the difference between defending against a claim and asserting a claim. To avoid any confusion, however, the Federal Rules require a plaintiff to file a reply only when the counterclaim in the defendant's answer is labeled "counterclaim." Otherwise, no reply is permitted. In *Rasmussen,* there was no suggestion that the accident was Anne's fault, so Paula did not file a counterclaim, and Anne did not file a reply.

6. DISCOVERY

a. The Discovery Devices

Prior to the Federal Rules, one party could not force the other to provide information concerning the case. A lawyer could only guess at the evidence she would face at trial, so preparation for trial was haphazard at best. Success at trial frequently turned on ambush, surprise, and an attorney's skill at reacting to the unexpected, rather than the merits of the case.

The Federal Rules changed all that. The Rules provided a comprehensive set of discovery devices, which made it possible for each side to learn about the other side's witnesses, documents, and theories of the case. The following are the formal discovery devices provided by the Federal Rules:

i. Depositions (Fed. R. Civ. P. 30)

A deposition is a formal, oral examination of a potential witness by an attorney for one of the parties. The attorney who wishes to examine a particular person will schedule the deposition, typically at her own office, will notify the other party, and will subpoena the witness. At the scheduled time, a court reporter will administer an oath to the witness, and the deposing attorney will then question the witness, in much the same fashion as would occur at trial. The court reporter will record the testimony stenographically (as if at a trial). The attorney for the other side will state objections when she considers it appropriate; these objections will be noted by the reporter, but the witness is ordinarily required to answer the question despite the objection. After the deposing attorney has completed her examination of the witness, the opposing attorney may cross examine the witness. After the deposition, the reporter will prepare a "verbatim" (word-for-word) transcript of the questions, answers, and objections.

Depositions are very useful. In contrast with written forms of discovery, the deposition witness has to answer question after question without consulting her attorney, so her answers are likely to be more revealing. Any new information which comes out can be immediately developed by more questioning. The deposing attorney sits face to face with the deponent, so that she can appraise the deponent as a potential witness, as well as develop a feel for the probity of her answers.

In addition to providing information, depositions can be useful at trial in two ways. First, if a witness lives a great distance from the place of trial, she can be deposed near her home and then the transcript of her testimony can be used at trial in lieu of her live testimony; this saves her the trip to the courthouse. Likewise, if testimony at trial would otherwise be too inconvenient for a witness, or if the witness disappears or dies before trial, her deposition testimony can be used as a substitute for her testimony at trial.

When (as is more usual) the deponent testifies at trial, the deposition transcript can be used to keep her trial testimony honest, or at least consistent. If a witness' testimony at trial is different from what she said at the deposition, her deposition answer can be read back to her (in front of the jury), and she can be asked to explain the difference. Needless to say, this is embarrassing and will cast doubt on her testimony. To avoid this embarrassment, most witnesses reread their deposition testimony before testifying and try to keep their trial testimony consistent with what they said at deposition.

ii. Interrogatories (Fed. R. Civ. P. 33)

Each party is allowed to serve another party written questions, which the served party must then answer, under oath and in writing. This device serves the same purposes as the deposition, though its use is limited to interrogating other parties. Interrogatories are less expensive for the parties than depositions because there is no need for a court reporter and because they usually consume less of the attorneys' time. But the answers to interrogatories will be framed by the party's attorney, so they are likely to be carefully hedged and not as useful as a witness' answers at a deposition. In one circumstance, however, this is an advantage; interrogatories can be used to require the other party's attorney to reveal her theories of the case, and to inquire into other matters within the attorney's (rather than the party's) knowledge.

iii. Production of documents and the subpoena duces tecum (Fed. R. Civ. P. 34, 45)

The attorney may wish to examine personally and to copy or photograph certain documents or things in the possession of another person. If that person is another party, the attorney need only serve the party with a request to produce the documents or things to be examined. If the documents or things are in the possession of a person who is not a party, then the attorney may have to obtain a subpoena duces tecum, which is an order issued by the clerk of the court requiring the person named in the subpoena to produce certain described items.

iv. Physical and mental examinations (Fed. R. Civ. P. 35)

Under certain circumstances, a party can require another party to submit to a physical or mental examination by a physician chosen by the first party. If, for example, Wilton believed that Anne was exaggerating her injuries, he would be able to have her examined by a physician of his choice.

v. Requests for admission (Fed. R. Civ. P. 36)

A party may serve "requests for admission" upon another party. A requested admission is simply a statement that is considered admitted if it is not denied within 30 days. If a party denies a requested admission, and it is later determined that there were not reasonable grounds for that denial, the party may be required to pay the costs of proving that which should have been admitted.

This device is primarily useful for discovering which issues are actually going to be contested and disposing of the others. For example, the answer in *Rasmussen v. Graham* denied all items of damage, which means, as a theoretical matter, that Hart will have to prove each and every item at trial. As to some items, however, it is likely that there will be no real contest. Item 3 of the complaint lists a number of specific expenditures. If Hart wanted to get these out of the way in advance of the trial, he might submit requests for admissions. As to each item he would request separate admissions that the amount stated was the amount actually charged, that the amount charged was a reasonable charge for the particular service rendered, and that the service rendered was required as a result of the injuries Anne received in the accident. He would also enclose copies of each bill, and might request that Paula admit that each copy was a genuine copy of the original bill sent to Anne. Unless Wilton had some basis to doubt the propriety of any of the expenditures, he would allow them to be admitted. These admissions would mean that no further proof of those items would be required. Of course, the admissions would not establish Paula's responsibility for the injuries, and Anne would have to establish that crucial point before recovering for the listed expenditures. As a tactical matter, Hart might prefer to prove each bill at trial, on the theory that this will help impress upon the jury the seriousness of Anne's injuries and thereby might increase the amount the jury awards for Anne for her "pain and suffering."

b. Controlling Discovery: Discovery Plan and Scheduling Order

The discovery devices provided by the Federal Rules gives attorneys powerful means of probing each other's case. Unfortunately, full use of these devices can become overwhelmingly expensive. Depositions, for example, eat up a huge amount of attorney time. Prior to each deposition, each party's attorney must thoroughly prepare. For the deposing attorney, this means trying to anticipate all lines of questioning that she might want to cover in the trial and preparing lines of questions to cover every area within the deponent's knowledge, because she will not be permitted to depose the same witness twice. For the defending attorney, preparation for the deposition requires preparation of the witness for the rigors of the deposition. The attorney must anticipate all likely lines of questioning and go over each with the witness so that the witness is prepared to give honest but minimally damaging answers. Frequently the witness must be taken through a mock deposition, so that she can be made aware of the perils of giving careless or even just casual answers to the deposing attorney. Finally, the deposition itself will consume hours, perhaps days, of attorney time for both parties.

Interrogatories can impose a great burden on the party who must answer them. An interrogatory in a commercial case, for example, might ask the party to list daily receipts at each of a number of stores over a period of a number of years, or to identify by name and address each and every person who had ever complained or otherwise commented upon a particular product. Similarly, responding to a request for production might require a party to collect thousands of documents for inspection by the opposing party.

Until recently, discovery was subjected to very little control by the judges. Physical examinations could only be required with the permission of the judge, but all the other devices were invoked at will by each of the attorneys. A party who felt unreasonably overburdened by the other party's discovery demands could request a protective order from the judge, but she was not likely to get relief from any but the most egregious abuses. The prevailing tendency was to encourage the free use of discovery. This made it possible for parties to use discovery as a potent weapon — forcing settlements, delaying trial, or increasing the burden of litigating so that a potential plaintiff might decide it just wasn't worth filing the action in the first place.

There has been a great deal of debate about the appropriate remedy for these problems. Major steps were taken in 1991 and 1993, when the Supreme Court and Congress adopted significant amendments to the discovery provisions of the Federal Rules. These changes limited the number of depositions, interrogatories, and requests for admission, required the development of an orderly discovery plan by the parties, required the voluntary disclosure of substantial information at the beginning of discovery, and increased attorneys' responsibilities to proceed only in good faith.

Hart and Wilton were operating under Colorado's version of the amended rules — substantially identical, for our purposes, to the Federal Rules. Under Rule 26(f), within 75 days of Wilton's first response (his motion to dismiss), Hart and Wilton were required to meet face to face and to discuss "the nature and basis of their claims and defenses and the possibilities for a prompt settlement or resolution of the case, ... and to develop a proposed discovery plan."

The Rule 26(f) Discovery Plan should include the following details:[6]

Whether the parties request a conference with the judge prior to entry of the scheduling order;

whether settlement of the case is likely, and what alternative procedures might facilitate settlement;

the date for exchanging "disclosures" (discussed below);

the dates for beginning and for completing all discovery,

the dates for exchange of written reports from each party's expert witnesses;

the subjects on which discovery will be permitted;

the maximum number of interrogatories, requests for admission, and depositions;

the maximum length of depositions;

the date for filing "dispositive motions" (i.e., motions which would terminate all or part of the case);

the date for filing lists of witnesses and exhibits;

the date for objecting to the other side's witnesses and exhibits;

the estimated length and proposed date for the trial; and

whether the parties request a conference with the judge shortly before the trial (a "pretrial conference").

Where the attorneys cannot agree on a particular item, the Plan includes a separate statement from each attorney on that item.

The parties file the Discovery Plan with the court. The judge assigned to the case will then enter a scheduling order to control the subsequent development of the case. Ordinarily, the judge will accept the dates and other provisions agreed

---

[6]The amendments which provided for the Rule 26(f) discovery plan also provided a sample of such a plan, which is included in the official forms following the Federal Rules, as Form 35. Form 35 identifies by example the details to be included in a discovery plan.

to by the parties. Where the parties could not agree, or if the schedule agreed to is too slow for the judge's liking, she will generally hold a scheduling conference with the attorneys (typically by telephone) to iron out the details. Within a week or two she will issue a scheduling order, which will bind the parties throughout the rest of the case (absent demonstration of "good cause" for modification).

c. The Rule 26(f) Meeting in *Rasmussen v. Graham*

Shortly after receiving Wilton's initial response to the Complaint (Defendant's Motion to Dismiss), Hart phoned Wilton to discuss the case. (This, of course, was before Judge Shannon's ruling on the motion and before Wilton filed Defendant's Answer to the Complaint.) Hart and Wilton had both been practicing law in Fort Collins for a number of years, and had a cordial professional relationship as is common among attorneys in small and mid-sized communities. After exchanging pleasantries, Wilton expressed some sympathy for Anne's condition and asked how she was doing. This led, rather naturally, to a discussion of settlement in which Wilton made clear Safeco's reluctance to settle.

Hart and Wilton then discussed scheduling the Rule 26(f) meeting. As discussed above, the rules required that they meet within 75 days of Wilton's motion. Hart had two weeks to file his brief opposing Wilton's Motion to Dismiss, and Wilton would then have one week to file a reply. Even if Judge Shannon scheduled oral argument, the motion was likely to be decided within three weeks after Wilton's reply. Finally, Wilton would be required to file Defendant's Answer within 10 days of Judge Shannon's ruling on his motion. Hart and Wilton agreed that it would be preferable to have the meeting after Judge Shannon had ruled on the motion and Wilton had answered the complaint, so that they could have a clearer idea of the issues remaining to be litigated. Consulting their calendars, they agreed on a date about 65 days after the date of Wilton's motion — which still left them a 10-day safety margin.

As discussed in prior sections, Judge Shannon granted Wilton's motion, dismissing the claims against Roger Graham, and Wilton filed his answer, setting out Paula's guest statute defense. On the agreed upon date, Hart and Wilton met at Wilton's office. They started, once again, by discussing the possibility of settlement. Based on discussions with Wilton, Safeco had a great deal of confidence in the guest statute defense. Their offer remained the same.

Hart and Wilton then turned to scheduling discovery. This appeared to both to be a fairly straightforward case to develop. There were not a large number of witnesses, and the factual issues were fairly straightforward. Neither Hart nor Wilton felt a need for special limitations or protections in discovery, and they agreed that the issues raised by the guest statute would control the outcome of the case. Consulting their calendars, they were able to work out a proposed schedule for discovery and for the trial of the case. Finally, they agreed to request a pre-trial conference with Judge Shannon approximately 10 days prior to the trial.

Wilton agreed to prepare a draft Discovery Plan for Hart's agreement. Two days later Wilton faxed Hart a draft, which Hart accepted and filed with the court. One week later Judge Shannon issued a scheduling order requiring the parties to comply with that Discovery Plan.

d. The Parties' Initial Disclosure Statements

Under the 1993 amendments, parties are required to exchange three separate sets of disclosure statements: "Initial Disclosures" at the outset of discovery (within 10 days of the Rule 26(f) discovery planning meeting), "Disclosure of Expert Testimony" 90 days prior to trial, and "Pretrial Disclosures" 30 days prior to trial. The initial disclosure requirement is a major change in the pretrial discovery process.

Rule 26(a)(1), the Initial Disclosure rule, requires four types of information to be included in the initial disclosure statement:

(A) The name, address and telephone number of every person likely to have information concerning issues raised by the pleadings;

(B) A copy or a description of every document, computer record or other physical item within the possession or control of the party which is relevant to the issues raised by the pleadings;

(C) An explanation of how each claim for damages was calculated;

(D) A copy of applicable insurance policies.

The third and fourth of these requirements are relatively straightforward, and not very different from the usual prior practice. The first and second requirements, however, impose substantial obligations on attorneys for litigants. Formerly, information had to be revealed to the other side only pursuant to appropriate demands. In the typical lawsuit, each party would send the other interrogatories requesting a list of persons having any information concerning the issues of the case, and a list of all documents (etc.) having relevance to the issues of the case. A party would only have to provide such information, however, if the interrogatory was very specific in its description of each issue. Thus, if an interrogatory asked your client for a list of every document "relevant to disputed facts alleged with particularity in the pleadings of this case" (roughly the language of the new rule), you could respond with an objection that the interrogatory was not sufficiently specific; it was the responsibility of the discovering party to identify particular "disputed facts" before you could be required to identify which documents were relevant to those facts.

The trial process is contentious and highly adversarial. Although Hart and Wilton, as members of a small local bar, managed to get along reasonably well as individuals, there was no doubt that they usually represented opposite sides of painful and frequently bitter disputes. Each saw his first priority as the zealous (but necessarily ethical) representation of his client. For each, help to the

contentious - strife; dispute

opponent was almost always harm to his own client. Thus, discovery itself worked against the adversarial grain of these attorneys. When a discovery request was made, it was understood that the natural response of every attorney would be to read the request as narrowly as possible, and to give only the information literally and necessarily required by the language of the request. Documents relevant to particular facts would be identified and described only if those facts were set out specifically and unavoidably in the discovery request (i.e., the interrogatory). A request for the identity of all documents relevant to the "disputed facts alleged with particularity in the pleadings" would not be nearly specific enough to require compliance. The recipient would simply object to the interrogatory as overbroad, and otherwise ignore it.

The 1993 amendments reflected an effort to deal with the "cat and mouse" nature of adversarial discovery. The disclosure requirement is an attempt to foster a full exchange of information at the beginning of discovery, as opposed to the former practice, which forced production of information only after a battle regarding the specificity and accuracy of the particular requests. The notes of the committee which drafted the rules emphasized that the rules appealed to attorneys' obligations as "officers of the court," and that attorneys must disclose information and documents which the opposing side would find useful for the preparation and presentation of its case. Substantial sanctions are available against both the attorney and her client for breach of this obligation.

The initial disclosure statements for Hart and Wilton were relatively straightforward. Both parties listed Paula and Anne, Dr. and Mrs. Graham, the patrolman called to the accident, and the driver of the road maintainer as persons with knowledge of relevant, disputed issues. Hart also listed Anne's family, her doctors, and others with knowledge of her injuries. For relevant documents and physical items, both listed the accident report, accident scene photographs, and related documents; Hart also listed various medical records and bills, as well as pre-accident and post-accident pictures of Anne showing effects of the accident on her appearance. Regarding calculation of damages, Hart's statement listed Anne's medical expenses to the date of the statement, and described generally other categories of damages which Hart expected to prove at trial; Hart did not need to be specific, because the complaint had not been specific. Finally, Wilton's disclosure statement included a copy of Paula's insurance policy.

The parties were now ready for discovery.

7. THE IMPACT OF DISCOVERY ON THE DEVELOPMENT OF *RASMUSSEN v. GRAHAM*

Once the answer was received, and indeed from the very beginning of the case, it was obvious to both Hart and Wilton that the guest statute posed the major obstacle to Anne's recovery. If there were no guest statute, Anne would have to prove only that Paula had committed an act of simple negligence. Paula had

33

driven her car into the rear end of a large, highly visible object, so Anne would probably have had little trouble convincing a jury that Paula had been guilty of simple negligence.

So, for Anne to recover, Hart had to deal with the guest statute. Put yourself in Hart's place: What must you prove for Anne to recover? Let's examine the language of the guest statute again:

> *Guest has no cause of action — when.* — No person transported by the owner or operator of a motor vehicle as his guest, without payment for such transportation, shall have a cause of action for damages against such owner or operator for injury, death or loss in case of accident, unless such accident shall have been intentional on the part of such owner or operator or caused by his intoxication, or by negligence consisting of a willful and wanton disregard of the rights of others ....

You will note that the basic part of the statute provides that "no person transported by the ... operator of a motor vehicle as his guest ... shall have a cause of action for damages against such ... operator." But the statute, by its terms, also provides two situations in which a guest's recovery would not be precluded.

First, the statute applies only if plaintiff was transported "as his guest, *without payment* for such transportation..." [Emphasis added]. Thus, if there was "payment" (whatever that might mean) for the transportation, Anne's cause of action is not precluded by the statute.

Second, the statute applies "*unless* such accident shall have been [1] intentional on the part of such owner ... or [2] caused by his intoxication, or [3] by negligence consisting of a willful and wanton disregard of the rights of others ..." [Emphasis and numbering added]. If Anne can bring this case within any of the three situations included within the "unless" clause, the statute will not preclude her from recovering. There is no suggestion that the accident was either intentional on the part of Paula or due to her intoxication. Were Paula's acts "negligence consisting of a willful and wanton disregard of the rights of others"? If so, then Anne's cause of action is not precluded by the statute.

The case, then, turns on two terms: "payment" and "willful and wanton." If Hart can prove either term applicable, Anne will recover. For Wilton to prevail, it must be determined that neither term is applicable. What are Anne's chances for recovery? That depends on two things: what each "exception" means, and whether the facts of the case are such that meaning is satisfied.

On the basis of what he knew about the case, Hart felt that Anne stood a chance on both theories. As we shall see, each was pursued at trial. But for simplicity's sake we will concentrate on the term "payment" in the next section.

QUESTIONS

1. What does "payment" mean? Does the statute define "payment"? Does it even suggest a meaning for the term?

2. If "payment" includes providing company for the operator, a guest would almost always prevail, and the statute would almost never be applicable. Do you find any language in the statute that precludes this interpretation? Is there any reason not to interpret the statute in this fashion?

3. If something more than merely providing company for the operator is required for "payment" within the meaning of the statute, what is it?

a. Depositions in General

At an early stage in the case, Hart thought Anne might well be able to show sufficient "payment." Wilton, on the other hand, saw the matter differently: He felt Anne's position on this issue was so weak that the court ought to take the issue out of the case by ruling in advance of trial that no payment had been made. How could two conscientious professionals differ so completely in what appears to be such a cut-and-dried issue? As you will see, in this business issues are seldom cut-and-dried.

Wilton wanted the "payment" issue out of the case. His first step was to identify the evidence that Hart would use to argue in favor of "payment." That evidence would most likely consist of the testimony of Anne and Paula. After talking extensively with Paula, Wilton knew what she would say during her testimony. Wilton's next step was to depose Anne. Shortly after Judge Shannon issued his scheduling order, Wilton mailed the following Notice of Deposition to Hart (with the original being mailed to the clerk of the court to become a part of the court record in this case).

IN THE DISTRICT COURT

IN AND FOR THE COUNTY OF LARIMER

AND STATE OF COLORADO

Division I

Civil Action No. 20395

ANNE RASMUSSEN,	)	
	)	
Plaintiff,	)	
	)	
vs.	)	NOTICE OF TAKING
	)	DEPOSITION
PAULA GRAHAM and ROGER GRAHAM,	)	
	)	
Defendants.	)	

TO: Plaintiff, Anne Rasmussen

You are hereby notified that you must appear for the taking of your deposition at the office of Alfred Wilton, [address omitted], at 3:00 PM on March 15, 1995, before Gilbert I. Davenport, Certified Shorthand Reporter and Deputy Clerk of the District Court, which deposition will be taken pursuant to the Colorado Rules of Civil Procedure, and at which time and place you must be present.

February 9, 1995

[Signed] Alfred Wilton
Attorney for Defendant
[Address and Telephone Omitted]

Hart, of course, had talked extensively with Anne, but he needed to hear what Paula's testimony was going to be. So, upon receiving the notice of Anne's deposition, he telephoned Wilton and arranged that Hart would take Paula's deposition, in Wilton's office, immediately following Wilton's deposition of Anne. To keep the court's file complete, Hart mailed a Notice of Deposition of Paula to the clerk's office, with a copy to Wilton.

b. The Deposition of the Plaintiff

i. The "payment" issue

At the appointed time, Anne, Hart, and the court reporter appeared at Wilton's office. As a named party, Paula had the right to be present, but Hart and Wilton had agreed that Paula would not attend Anne's deposition, and Anne would not attend Paula's. After the court reporter administered the oath to Anne, Wilton commenced his questioning.

First he established certain personal information, such as Anne's full name, age, address, and so on. The following is a transcript of some of the questions and answers that followed. As you read the transcript, see if you can keep track of what Wilton is trying to get Anne to say and why.

Q: (by Wilton) First of all, I would like to review your friendship with Paula Graham. You have indicated that you met her as a sophomore at Fort Collins High School?

A: (by Anne) Yes.

Q: And that you became acquainted with her on a better basis when you were juniors and seniors?

A: Yes.

Q: And during the junior year you became better friends?

A: Yes.

Q: I am going to ask you to put it into words what you meant by the fact that during your junior year you became better friends. What did you mean by that?

A: Well, it is hard to put in words. We were acquaintances when we were sophomores and at the beginning of our junior year. We never had been like best friends, like I have known all my life or anything. I don't remember exactly when we started doing things together but then we used to go to football games and stuff like that.

Q: Were you with other friends, too?

A: Yes.

Q: Now, this accident happened during your senior year?

A: Yes.

Q: If I understand it correctly, you maintained your friendship up until that time anyway?

A: Yes.

Q: Did the friendship involve visiting back and forth in each other's houses?

A: Yes.

Q: Did you ever stay overnight at the Graham house?

A: Yes.

Q: About how many times?

A: I couldn't say exactly.

Q: Can you approximate how many times you stayed over there?

A: I would say five times. I mean I can't tell you exactly how many times I spent over there.

Q: And you went on trips together, as I understand your testimony, three or four times?

A: Yes.

Q: Was this just the two of you?

A: I don't remember if all the trips were just us. But several times we went together alone.

Q: Just the two of you?

A: Yes.

Q: And these trips, were these during the junior or senior year?

A: We probably started going places the summer of our junior year.

Q: You just continued on?

A: Yes.

Q: Let's get into the area involving the trip. If I understand it correctly, you knew that Paula had a car to drive around?

A: Yes.

Q: And that in driving around town there was never any conversation about, that is, in Fort Collins there was never any conversation about paying for the gas or anything like that, was there?

A: No.

Q: You said you went on three or four or five trips during your senior or junior year, is that correct?

A: Correct.

Q: Now, because you were friends, I assume that you offered to pay half the gas if you rode with her. Is that correct?

A: Well, I don't know if I offered to pay gas. It was understood that I had to pay. She had to pay for her gas and if we went on a trip I had to pay half of it.

Q: You had to?

A: I don't know if she wouldn't have taken me if I hadn't. She didn't say. But if I didn't have the money I would have gotten it from my father. That is the way we did it.

Q: You were friends?

A: Yes, I said we were friends.

Q: And she never told you couldn't go if you didn't pay her?

A: It never came up that I didn't pay her.

Q: Now, on the trip that we have in question, as far as the payment of any money on the trip, that involved the trip from Fort Collins to Steamboat that we are talking about in this case, you never at any time ever did pay her any money?

A: No. But you know I was supposed to pay her.

Q: I will get to that in a minute.

A: No.

Q: And she never asked you for any money at any time did she on this trip?

A: No, in answer to your question.

Q: But you understood that on the return trip you would pay for half of the gas or something like that. Is that correct?

A: We discussed it. It was not just understood. If you mean that we didn't talk about it.

Q: Let's talk about the trip then. Was the idea of the trip that you were going up to stay at the Graham trailer as a guest of Dr. and Mrs. Graham?

A: Yes.

Q: It wasn't expected that you pay any expenses at the trailer or anything like that?

A: No.

Q: It wasn't expected that you buy any portion of the food or anything at the trailer?

A: No.

Q: You went along as a friend of Paula's. Isn't that correct?

A: Correct.

Q: How did you get to Steamboat Springs?

A: We drove up in Paula's car.

Q: Is that the Tercel?

A: Yes.

Q: Who was with you in Paula's car when you went over to Steamboat Springs from Fort Collins?

A: Just Paula and I.

Q: And when was this in relation to the accident?

A: I think we went up two days before the accident. That would have been the 28th, I think.

Q: Where did you join Paula, to make the trip?

A: I think she picked me up, at my house.

Q: Do you remember what time that was?

A: It was in the morning. About ten-thirty or eleven. I'm not sure.

Q: After Paula picked you up, where did you go?

A: Back to Paula's. She remembered something she forgot.

Q: Then where did you go?

A: The Gasamat. We went to the Gasamat.

Q: What is the Gasamat, Anne?

A: That's a gas station where the gas pumps work by tokens. You buy these tokens for two dollars each, and then you use them to operate the pumps. Paula always got her gas there.

Q: Who paid for the gasoline?

A: Paula did. You see, the day we left she had four Gasamat tokens she got for Christmas from a friend she drove to school. We went by the Gasamat and she said she would put her tokens in. We didn't know if there would be a Gasamat up there. And I would pay the gas on the way back.

Q: Do you recall how long it took you to get to Steamboat?

A: Approximately five hours, I would say.

Q: Did you have any trouble going up?

A: No.

Q: After you got to Steamboat Springs, where did you go?

A: To Paula's trailer, her parents' trailer.

Q: Were her parents already there?

A: Yes.

Q: Had they arrived before you two arrived?

A: Yes.

Q: I see. When you got to Steamboat Springs that day, did you do any skiing on the day of the 28th?

A: No.

Q: What did you do, if you recall?

A: Do you know what day that was?

Q: It would have been a Sunday.

A: I don't recall, except for we spent the night in their trailer.

Q: Were you there the next day also, the 29th?

A: Yes.

Q: Do you recall what you did the day of the 29th?

A: I don't really remember. We went downtown to visit some people.

Q: Did you do any skiing on the day of the 29th?

A: No.

Q: You were over there at Steamboat to ski, I assume?

A: Yes, except for, yes. Well, can I explain this?

Q: Yes.

A: Paula had mono at the time, and I brought my skis, and she wasn't able to ski, really, and I was going to ski the next day. Well, I was going to ski some, but she couldn't ski.

Q: I see. Although her skis were there?

A: Uh-huh, yes.

Q: So because of her mono you did not go skiing that next day, the 29th, a Monday?

A: Yes.

Q: Where did you stay that evening of the 29th?

A: At Paula's trailer.

Q: That particular evening did you party at all?

A: I remember we had some friends with us. We went to the ski lodge, I think. I can't remember exactly the nights we did these things, but not really partied, I don't think.

Q: Well, how late were you out, do you recall, on the evening of the 29th of December, 1980.

A: We were probably in before midnight.

Q: The next morning, did you go skiing?

A: No.

Q: The morning of December 30?

A: No.

Q: What did you do?

A: We got up. We went into town, Steamboat, and then I would say at approximately ten o'clock we went to Craig.

Q: You mentioned that on the date of the 29th of December you went to town also. Where is the Graham trailer in relation to Steamboat Springs?

A: Well, it's between Craig and Steamboat Springs, only it's really in Steamboat Springs. I mean, it's between. Do you know what I mean? I don't know the exact mileage out of Steamboat Springs, or even if it's out of Steamboat Springs, except it's on the outskirts.

Q: On the west side of town?

A: I don't know my directions.

Q: Toward Craig?

A: Towards Craig.[7]

Q: Is it necessary to drive to get to downtown Steamboat Springs?

A: Yes.

Q: When you went to downtown Steamboat Springs on the 29th and on the 30th again, whose car did you go in?

A: Paula's.

Q: You had driven with her then on the way over to Steamboat, and then on the 29th and 30th you had also driven with her around Steamboat?

A: Yes.

Q: On the evening of the 29th, when you went out, did you also drive with her?

A: Yes. The whole trip I drove with her.

Q: Now, Anne, while you were up there the weather was very cold, wasn't it?

A: Yes.

---

[7] Craig is approximately 42 miles west of Steamboat Springs.

Q: And is it your memory, that on the morning of the 30th, only the Tercel would start?

A: I think that's right. But I don't know for sure.

Q: Do you remember Dr. Graham taking this 1987 Tercel to downtown Steamboat, to get jumper cables for the car that wouldn't start?

A: He took it. I don't know if he took it downtown. I didn't see him take it or anything, but he took it.

Q: When Dr. Graham took the Tercel on the morning of the 30th, didn't he fill it with gas?

A: I don't know.

Q: Wasn't the Tercel's gas tank full when you left Steamboat that morning to drive to Craig?

A: I don't know. I don't remember.

Q: You didn't have any conversation relating to driving, payment for driving around Steamboat Springs, did you?

A: The whole trip was included in it.

Q: I am asking you?

A: What do you mean by that question?

Q: Did you have any conversation relating to paying for gas while driving around Steamboat Springs?

A: No. She didn't need any. If she had, I would have paid it.

Q: Do you know?

A: No, because she paid on the way up.

Q: It wasn't because Dr. Graham filled the car up with gas?

A: It could have been.

Q: Now on the way over from Steamboat to Craig you went along as a friend of Paula's, to accompany her on this trip to get this key, correct?

A: Right.

Q: You just went along for the ride, if I understand it correctly?

A: Correct.

Q: In other words, you didn't have any business in Craig yourself?

A: Well, I didn't buy anything.

Q: Did Paula need your help on the trip to Craig?

A: No.

Q: Did you help her on the trip?

A: I don't know what you mean?

Q: Did you give her directions?

A: No.

Q: Did you help her find the hardware store?

A: I don't remember.

Q: Did you pay for the key?

A: No.

Q: You went along simply for the company?
A: That's right.

QUESTIONS

1. Was Anne surprised by these questions, or had she thought about them in advance? As Anne's attorney, how should Hart have prepared Anne for this deposition? Ethically, what should Hart be permitted to do, and what should he be prohibited from doing. For example, which of the following practices would you consider appropriate? Borderline? Inappropriate?

1. Telling Anne that she would be deposed, explaining the procedure, and telling her that Wilton would cover a number of subjects including the issue of "payment," but not going over her answers with her, and not explaining the legal significance of "payment"?

2. Explaining the significance of "payment" *after* having a detailed discussion with Anne about the facts of the case, and then:

a. Helping her change her story to match what is needed under the statute?

b. Allowing her to change her story on her own, but not giving her any help?

c. Not allowing her to change the facts of her story, but taking her through a mock deposition with these questions (over and over) and helping her plan the language of her answers to the likely questions?

d. Asking her the likely questions, but not telling her which of her answers were more helpful to her case, and which were damaging?

3. Before having a detailed discussion with Anne about the events of the case, explaining to her in detail the significance of her answers about "payment," and telling her to think about that carefully for a few days before she discusses the facts of the case with Hart? If that is ethical, which of the practices described in the preceding paragraph should be permitted?

As Anne's attorney, which would you want to do? Which would you permit yourself to do? Would your answer to either of these questions be affected by the fact that your fee for the case was a percentage of her ultimate recovery?

2. What has Wilton established by this testimony? Have Anne's answers helped Paula's case or her own? Are there any questions you would have liked to ask about the subjects he covered?

3. What facts do you see that would support an inference of "payment"? What facts were developed in the deposition to support an inference of "no payment"?

4. Do you think that there was "payment" within the meaning of the statute? If not, do you think that a reasonable person could believe there was payment?

ii. The accident

Wilton also questioned Anne closely about the accident itself. The following is an exchange that proved important at the trial:

Q: (by Wilton) Now, Anne, I would like you to describe to me the best you can recall just what happened right before the accident.

A: (by Anne) The way I remember it, we came, you know, part of the way was winding, you know. I don't remember passing hardly any traffic, or there being any traffic. I remember going around a curve to the left, and then we were in a straightaway, sort of a downgrade. Not really straight. But, well, this is getting to the accident.

Q: Fine. That's fine.

A: We were going down this hill. It wasn't really a hill. It was a grade, and there was a snowplow on the road, on our side of the road in front of us quite a ways away. I don't know the feet or anything. But then, see, there was a little curve to the right. There was a truck coming along the curve on the other side of the road towards us, which, so, since that truck was coming we just went into the back of the snowplow.

Q: When you were going around the curve to the left, could you see the snowplow ahead of you?

A: Not yet.

Q: Was there a —

A: It was right after we came out of it, probably.

Q: Did the curve to the left involve also going up an incline of some sort?

A: I can't really say. If it was, it wasn't a great one.

Q: Was it sufficient to block the view of what was ahead of you, particularly the snowplow?

A: We didn't see the snowplow until we were out of the curve.

Q: And then you were coming down an incline? Is that what I understand?

A: A slight incline. It wasn't like that (indicating).

Q: Well, some incline?

A: Okay.

Q: Okay. And the road curved again?

A: I am talking about when I saw the curve to the right, that is the curve we never got to.

Q: I see.

A: See, we ran into the snowplow before we got to this curve (indicating).

Q: Can you say how far ahead of your car the snowplow was when you first saw the snowplow?

A: I have no — I can't tell in feet. Can you give me an estimation that I could go by?

Q: Well, anything that would help you understand distance, if you can put it in terms that would mean something to you.

A: Okay. A city block. Is that good enough?

Q: All right. Now, so I can find out what you mean by "a city block," one like we have in downtown Fort Collins?

A: Yes.

Q: All right. Now, at the point that you first saw the snowplow, did you say anything to Paula then?

A: I don't recall what we said. We looked at each other. I mean, we acknowledged, we both knew that we saw it.

Q: Did Paula attempt to slow the speed of the vehicle?

A: I don't know.

Q: Did you see her depress the brake pedal?

A: No.

Q: What did you do as far as where you were sitting in the car after the time you first saw the snowplow ahead of you?

A: Just sat there and watched. I mean, we knew there was a pretty good chance, and I just waited, because it wasn't really that long.

Q: How long was it?

A: Well, you know, I can't say exactly. It seemed like quite awhile, a few minutes. It might not have been that long.

After Wilton finished his questioning, Hart was permitted to ask Anne questions concerning any of the territory covered by Wilton's questions. Hart asked just a few questions, to clear up an ambiguity that had developed. Wilton could have resumed limited questioning at that point, but chose not to, and Anne's deposition was over.

c. The Deposition of Defendant Paula Graham

As agreed, Hart then deposed Paula. It turned out that Paula's deposition was not as important as Anne's, and we will not discuss it further.

That was about all there was by way of formal discovery. Most of the additional information each attorney needed had been included in the initial disclosure statements, or was available through informal discovery. At this point, the attorneys were nearly ready for trial.

8. SUMMARY JUDGMENT

a. Summary Judgment in General

Before the advent of discovery, the only real way to test whether there was evidence to support the allegations of the pleadings was to take the case to trial. But discovery changed that. Through discovery, attorneys can get a fairly clear picture of each other's evidence. At times that evidence is so lacking that trial will be a waste of time. At the close of evidence in these cases, the judge will rule that there was not enough evidence to permit a verdict for that party. (Such a ruling is called a directed verdict, or an order for judgment as a matter of law.)

If an attorney believes that the other side's evidence is so weak that a directed verdict will be ordered at the close of evidence, she may file a motion for summary judgment. This is a procedure for showing in advance of trial that the other side's evidence on a particular issue is too weak to justify trial of that issue; if the motion is granted, the moving party will be treated as though it had prevailed at trial on that issue.

To see how this works, suppose that Anne's parents also had a cabin in Steamboat Springs, but that Anne for one reason or another had been unable to ride up with her own parents. Suppose further that Anne called Paula and offered Paula twenty dollars if Paula would drive up to Steamboat Springs. If Paula accepted and the accident happened on the way up, then there could be little doubt that the twenty dollar payment would take the case out of the guest statute.

For our hypothetical, let's assume that Anne's complaint alleged the twenty dollar payment, and Paula's answer denied it. Based on the pleadings, there would appear to be a factual dispute as to "payment," and a motion to dispose of this issue on the pleadings would fail. But the facts revealed at deposition are frequently different (and of course more complete) than the facts alleged in the technical pleadings. Unless Paula lied at her deposition, her testimony would show facts so clearly establishing "payment" that a jury would be required to decide that payment had occurred. In other words, if *at trial* both Anne and Paula testified that there had been an agreement to pay twenty dollars for the trip and actual payment of that amount, Anne would be granted a directed verdict on that issue at the close of evidence. The summary judgment motion (including the deposition transcript) shows that Anne will be entitled to a directed verdict if the matter goes to trial, so the summary judgment motion will be granted.

It is conceivable, of course, that the jury would not believe Paula's and Anne's (hypothetical) testimony regarding the twenty dollar payment. After all, Paula and Anne are friends, and Paula probably feels terrible about the accident. If there was a payment, she would lose the case, and the insurance company (not Paula) would have to pay Paula's friend thousands of dollars — all at no cost to Paula. Paula might feel that the least she could do, after causing Anne so much trouble, would be to tell a small fib so that Anne could be paid by Safeco. Thus, a juror might suspect that Paula and Anne were lying, and that in fact there had not been any payment. Even so, the jury would probably still be required to accept the uncontroverted testimony that there had been a payment. In this hypothetical both Paula and Anne have sworn to the payment, and the only "evidence" against their testimony would be the jurors' suspicions. The judge would rule that "suspicion" is not enough evidence to support a finding of "no payment," and would direct a verdict in favor of Anne on the payment issue.

The procedure for filing a summary judgment motion is set out in Rule 56. In our hypothetical, Hart would simply submit the following papers:

1. A motion for summary judgment, which would be in substantially the same form as the motion to quash service, set out *supra.*

2. Hart's own affidavit, describing the circumstances under which Paula's and Anne's depositions were taken.

3. Excerpts from the depositions, showing the pertinent testimony.[8]

4. A memorandum or brief in support of the motion containing Hart's arguments as to why the attached documents show that Anne is entitled to a summary judgment on the payment issue.

Hart would mail the originals of these documents to the court, and would mail copies to Wilton. Wilton would be allowed a certain amount of time to produce affidavits and a memorandum to the contrary, and at a prearranged time Hart and Wilton would appear before the judge. Each attorney would have an opportunity to present his arguments on the matter, and the judge would then (or later) rule on the matter.

b. Allocation of Factfinding Functions Between Judge and Jury

It is often said that the credibility of witnesses is to be determined by the jury. But the preceding hypothetical shows that the jury's responsibility is closely supervised by the courts. Even though a reasonable person might have believed, after listening to Anne and Paula, that there simply had not been a twenty dollar agreement, most courts would require a jury to accept the testimony from the two friends. So even though Anne and Paula might each have constitutional or statutory guarantees of a right to a jury trial, that right is subject to substantial judicial control, particularly through summary judgment and directed verdict practice.

The right to a jury trial is a sensitive and important issue in American courts, and one on which attorneys strongly disagree. Some see juries as an important check on the power of judges and the government; this was clearly the view of many of the framers of the Constitution. Others see juries as capricious and

---

[8] Rule 56 also permits the use of an affidavit from a potential witness, showing that the affiant is competent to testify, and if called will testify at trial to particular facts. Thus, Hart could prepare an affidavit for Anne in which she would summarize her testimony regarding the twenty dollar payment and state that she will so testify. Hart could also prepare such an affidavit for Paula, but she is under no obligation to execute an affidavit for Hart, and so would not be likely to do so. Thus, friendly witness statements can be obtained for summary judgment motions by affidavit, but the statements of unfriendly witnesses will usually require depositions.

unpredictable, as well as inconvenient and expensive to use; this view was also held by some of the framers. This debate is reflected in summary judgment practice. At those times when juries are treasured, summary judgments are permitted only in the clearest of cases. But when juries fall into mild disfavor, summary judgments are granted more freely. The further development of *Rasmussen v. Graham* provides a clear demonstration of the relationship between the courts' attitude towards summary judgment and the parties' access to jury trial.

c. Summary Judgment in *Rasmussen v. Graham*

In the actual case, the facts pertaining to "payment" were not seriously in dispute. They were roughly as follows:

1. Anne and Paula usually shared the expense of buying gas for longer trips, but not for trips around town.

2. Paula frequently asked her passengers to "pay their share." She had testified that although a friend had given her the Gasamat tokens as a gift, she really believed that the friend owed her the tokens for trips they had previously taken together.

3. Paula testified that she liked to drive, but frequently had trouble coming up with gas money.

4. Paula had purchased the gas necessary to drive from Fort Collins to Steamboat Springs.

5. Anne had agreed to buy some gas for the return trip from Steamboat to Fort Collins.

6. There had been no explicit discussion, one way or the other, as to the purchase of gas to be used while driving around Steamboat, and while driving from Steamboat to Craig and back.

7. Anne had not yet purchased any gas; and,

8. After the trip from Fort Collins to Steamboat Springs Paula's father, not Anne, had bought gasoline for the Tercel.

9. Paula's mononucleosis meant that she could not ski and would therefore be alone (but for Anne) while her family was skiing. Further, Paula's plan to stay in Steamboat Springs after her parents returned to Fort Collins also meant that she would have been alone had Anne not come on the trip. Paula's mother had testified that she was not entirely comfortable with Paula's spending long periods of time alone in the trailer in Steamboat Springs.

Was Anne's pre-trip agreement to buy gas for the trip home "payment" within the meaning of the statute?

Let's ask the question slightly differently. Was her agreement to pay so clearly "payment" that a jury would be required to find in her favor after hearing the foregoing evidence? Or was her agreement (and the other circumstances described above) so clearly *not* "payment" that a jury would be required to find "no payment" and rule against Anne on this issue? Or was this a situation somewhere between these two extremes, in which the jury ought to be able to decide on its own whether or not Anne's promise was sufficient to constitute "payment" under the guest statute?

Wilton filed a summary judgment motion, arguing that under Colorado case law, the jury would not be permitted to find that Anne's social agreement to share expenses amounted to "payment." Therefore, he argued, summary judgment should be granted against Anne's first claim for relief. (If there were no "payment," Anne was within the guest statute and therefore could not recover for "simple" negligence (her first claim for relief), but still could recover if she showed "willful and wanton" negligence (her third claim).)

What is the meaning of "payment" as that word is used in the guest statute? At the close of the case, the jury will be told (under Colorado's official jury instructions) that "payment may be cash or any benefit which is sufficiently real, tangible or substantial so as to have been an inducing cause for the transportation." The central question in this case was whether a jury would be permitted to conclude that there was "payment" under this instruction. Could a jury reasonably conclude that Anne's promise to pay was a "real, tangible or substantial" benefit?

The meaning of language in a statute or an instruction is always open to dispute. Language cannot be so definite that its application will be clear in every circumstance. The meaning of language in statutes and instructions, however, is gradually made more precise and complete as the state's courts interpret the language.

In the years before the *Rasmussen* case, the Colorado Supreme Court had decided a number of cases dealing with the meaning of the word "payment." These cases are discussed more completely in a later section of this book, but we will consider some brief excerpts at this point. In one case (*Leoffler*) plaintiff was injured while on a trip with her fiance (defendant) and his family. The Court held that an alleged agreement to pay a carefully determined share of the expenses would not amount to "payment" because such compensation would be "merely incidental" and not "the moving influence for the transportation.... [T]he inducing cause of the transportation was the close friendship of the parties."

In *Mears*, plaintiff was in Grand Junction and his wife was hospitalized in Denver (200 miles away), so he asked defendant to drive him to Denver, in defendant's car. Plaintiff agreed to pay for all expenses of the trip, including fuel, food, and lodging, but would not otherwise compensate defendant for his time or for the use of his car. The Court held that plaintiff's agreement to pay expenses could not be "payment" under the statute. In so holding, it quoted with approval the following statements from cases decided in other states:

The courts have quite uniformly held that merely paying for gas and oil or sharing the payment for gas and oil is not of itself and alone sufficient to establish [payment].

[The facts] clearly show a situation of ... reciprocal hospitality and social courtesy between friends when the undertaking is for the mutual social pleasure of the parties.... The payment of certain traveling expenses by plaintiff ... amounted to nothing more than the exchange of social amenities.... Friendship and sociability were the basis of plaintiff's being in the car.

In *Folkers*, defendant was a commission salesman who took plaintiff, an important client, out for drinks and dinner, and was involved in an accident on the way to dinner. Defendant had testified that plaintiff's business was important to him, and that on the day in question he had initially gone over to plaintiff because he saw plaintiff talking with one of defendant's competitors. The Court still held that the purpose of the particular trip was primarily social, and that defendant's expectation of a business benefit was too indirect to constitute "payment."

In *Bridges*, the Court held that a cost sharing arrangement did amount to "payment." Plaintiff and defendant worked at the same place. In response to plaintiff's advertisement in the company bulletin, defendant and plaintiff agreed to share expenses for driving to work by driving (with the other as passenger) on alternate days. Plaintiff was injured while a passenger in defendant's car, and the Court held that the agreement to drive on alternate days *was* payment under the statute, because "the relationship [between plaintiff and defendant] was an impersonal one based upon business expediency and mutual benefit."

Finally, in *Burgoyne* the Colorado Court of Appeals held that a non-business arrangement could constitute "payment." Defendant was a sixteen year old with a learner's permit. Because he could not drive without a licensed adult in the car, he had asked plaintiff to accompany him. The Court held that plaintiff's presence in the car at defendant's request could provide a "material, substantial and tangible benefit" to defendant sufficient to constitute "payment." The Colorado Supreme Court ordered that the *Burgoyne* opinion be published, which conferred the status of "precedent" on the opinion; only about twenty percent of the Court of Appeals opinions were ordered to be published.

Wilton's motion for summary judgment gave Judge Shannon a great deal of trouble. After reading a number of Colorado Supreme Court opinions, including those discussed above, the judge granted the motion. Conceding that "payment" was ordinarily a question for the jury, he ruled that the evidence in this case fell within the Colorado Supreme Court opinions which limited the jury's ability to find "payment" in social situations. Judge Shannon entered an order dismissing Anne's first claim for relief. The guest statute applied, so Anne's only chance of recovering, as matters now stood, was to convince the jury that Paula acted with "willful and wanton disregard" of Anne's rights. Of the four theories articulated in Hart's original complaint, all but one had been dismissed.

QUESTIONS

1. Under the cases discussed above, what is the test for "payment"? Could a jury conclude that Anne's conduct met that test?

2. Reread the first six pages of Wilton's deposition of Anne (pp. 37-43, *supra*). Can you see how Wilton was trying to get Anne to testify in the language of the Colorado cases? This passage should bear out for you how a deposition is more of a weapon than an information gathering device; Wilton was obviously, and appropriately, trying to get Anne to admit facts which would entitle him to a summary judgment. In your opinion, did he succeed?

9. PRETRIAL CONFERENCE

The pretrial conference is a relatively recent development, gaining its first widespread acceptance in this country with the adoption of the Federal Rules in 1938. The manner in which it is used varies widely from court to court and from judge to judge, but it can be useful in the following ways:

a. Identifying issues apparently framed in the pleadings that are not really in dispute;

b. Providing definition for the issues that are left;

c. Giving each attorney and the court some notion of what the other side is planning;

d. Limiting the number of witnesses and the amount of documentary evidence; and

e. Providing the attorneys and the court with a blueprint for the trial.

The pretrial conference can also be used to explore the possibilities of a settlement of the case. By the time of the conference, each attorney knows (or should know) the strengths and weaknesses of the case, and has a fairly good idea of the strengths and weaknesses of the other side. Discussion of these matters in the presence of an impartial, knowledgeable outsider might lead the attorneys to common ground. If the judge agrees with the solution the attorneys settle on, the judge's agreement will help the attorneys sell the settlement to their clients. If the attorneys intend to discuss settlement, a separate judge will usually be provided so that the parties can talk candidly without fear of prejudicing the judge who will actually preside over the trial.

Thirty days prior to the scheduled first day of trial, Hart and Wilton exchanged pretrial disclosure statements. These statements listed all witnesses who might be called and all documents which might be introduced into evidence; if Hart or Wilton omitted a witness or document he intended to use at trial, he would be precluded from using that witness or document. Two weeks later, Hart and Wilton each filed their objections to the evidence listed in the other's pretrial disclosure statement; failure to raise an objection which could have been raised at that time would preclude the attorney from making that objection at trial. One week later the parties met with Judge Shannon in his chambers for the pretrial conference.

The judge started with a general discussion of the case. He then went through each attorney's list of witnesses in order to determine what contribution each witness would make to the trial. If he had found any whose testimony might be repetitive, that witness's testimony may be excluded. The two attorneys' lists, however, were fairly sparse, so there was no need for that.

Next, there was some discussion concerning certain X-rays Hart wished to use at the trial. Prior to introducing physical evidence into a trial, it is normally necessary for the proponent of that evidence to establish certain preliminary facts. In order to admit the X-rays at trial, Hart could be required to lay a rather elaborate foundation that would entail bringing a radiologist from Denver (where the X-rays had been taken) to Fort Collins. Hart had listed these X-rays in his pretrial disclosure statement, and Wilton had preserved his right to object to the X-rays in his response. After some discussion of the X-rays, Wilton agreed not to object to foundational testimony from Anne's family physician, who was going to testify anyway, in lieu of requiring a witness from the Denver hospital where the X-rays were taken.

Then Hart brought up a matter which had emerged during discovery. At the deposition of Anne, Wilton had devoted a great deal of attention to the fact that Anne had not been wearing her seatbelt at the time of the accident. As Hart read the Colorado Supreme Court cases on the matter, the fact that a plaintiff was not wearing a seatbelt at the time of injury was considered irrelevant to the issues properly in the trial. Accordingly, Hart requested that the court rule in advance of trial that Wilton not question Anne or any other witness about seatbelts. This request was made in the form of a *motion in limine* (literally, a "threshold" or "preliminary" motion), which was simply a written pretrial request for a ruling on evidence that might be introduced at trial. Judge Shannon heard argument from each attorney, and then ruled that Wilton would be prohibited from raising the seatbelt issue.

Finally, the judge went through the facts of the case with the attorneys, in order to isolate the factual areas actually in dispute.

Immediately after the conference the judge prepared the following document:

IN THE DISTRICT COURT

IN AND FOR THE COUNTY OF LARIMER

AND STATE OF COLORADO

Division I

Civil Action No. 20395

ANNE RASMUSSEN,
 	
     Plaintiff,
 	
vs.
 	
PAULA GRAHAM and ROGER GRAHAM,
 	
     Defendants.
	)
	)
	)
	)
	) PRETRIAL ORDER
	)
	)
	)
	)

Pursuant to Rule 16 of the Colorado Rules of Civil Procedure, on June 1, 1995, a pretrial conference was had in the above-captioned case, and the following is hereby ordered:

1. The following facts are admitted and require no proof at trial:

a. That the Court has jurisdiction of the parties and the subject matter herein.

b. That a collision occurred on December 30, 1993, between a 1987 Toyota Tercel being driven by defendant, Paula Graham, and a 1979 Colorado State Highway Department maintainer approximately five miles west of Milner, Colorado, on U.S. Highway 40 in the County of Routt.

c. That at the time and place of the collision plaintiff, Anne Rasmussen, was a passenger in the 1987 Toyota Tercel.

2. Ruling by the Court:

a. Defendant's motion for summary judgment is hereby granted; defendant's attorney is directed to prepare an appropriate order for the signature of the Court.

b. On plaintiff's motion *in limine*, the Court hereby rules that no reference shall be made and no question asked to elicit a reference to the use or availability of seatbelts at any time pertinent to this case.

c. The Court accepts the stipulation of both counsel that plaintiff may offer X-rays without testimony from the radiologist who took or supervised the taking of the X-rays.

3. Witnesses:

The witnesses at the trial shall be those named in the plaintiff's and defendant's Pretrial Memoranda, and no others except for rebuttal purposes.

4. Exhibits:

The exhibits at the trial shall be those listed in plaintiff's and defendant's Pretrial Memoranda and no others except for rebuttal purposes.

5. The following issues of law and fact remain to be litigated at the trial and no others:

a. Did the conduct of defendant Paula Graham constitute a willful and wanton disregard of the rights of plaintiff Anne Rasmussen?

b. If defendant's conduct did constitute a willful and wanton disregard of the rights of plaintiff, Anne Rasmussen, what damages, if any, did plaintiff incur as a result of said conduct by defendant?[9]

6. The case is set for trial to a jury of six, three days having been allowed, to wit: June 12, 13, and 14, 1995.

7. The foregoing admission having been made by the parties, and the parties having specified the foregoing issues of fact and law remaining to be litigated, this order shall supplement the pleadings and shall govern the cause of the trial of this course, unless modified to present manifest injustice.

Dated at Fort Collins, Colorado this 5th day of June, 1995.

BY THE COURT
John Shannon
District Judge

C. THE TRIAL

All possible steps had been taken. The parties, their families and attorneys had been unable to settle this dispute. And substantial pretrial efforts sharpened the dispute, but did not dispose of it. Trial was not to be avoided.

At one point in history, a dispute such as this might have been settled more directly. Anne's relatives, if they were upset enough, might have tried to visit upon Paula or her family injuries similar to Anne's. If Anne's family were strong enough, they could; if not, they would pay dearly for their efforts.

At a later period in history, Paula and Anne would simply have taken their dispute to a respected elder in their community. If the member were sufficiently respected and the community sufficiently supportive of the elder's function, the disputants and their families would accept the decision, and live with it and each other in harmony. Though not an ideal solution, it settled disputes with a minimum of cost.

A number of institutions have successively been substituted for the community elder. We have had religious courts, trial by battle, trial by ordeal, and that curious combination of the latter two, trial by jury. But through all of these refinements, the major goal — satisfying the disputants with a minimum of bloodshed — has remained largely the same. You might ask yourself throughout

---

[9] Note that, under this formulation of the issues, Anne will receive damages only if she can show "willful and wanton disregard"; as a result of the judge's ruling that payment had not been made, Anne cannot recover damages caused by Paula's simple negligence.

our discussion, and throughout your professional career, just how well these procedures serve that goal, what other goals should be served by a judicial system, and how well our system is serving those other goals.

On Monday, June 12, 1995, after months of skirmishing, the day for trial finally arrived. By 9:00 A.M., the parties and their attorneys were in the court room, unpacked and ready to go.

During the week preceding trial, a deputy clerk had contacted about twenty residents of Larimer County (selected at random) and had instructed them that it was their time to serve their community as jurors. They, too, arrived at 9:00 A.M. Also present were the many persons needed by the court for the conduct of its business: clerks, the bailiff, court reporters, and the sheriff and deputy sheriffs. Also in attendance were Paula's and Anne's families, a few friends, and a few of the idle and the curious. All assembled to witness or participate in the resolution of Paula's and Anne's dispute.

At 9:05 A.M., Wilton, Hart, and a court reporter retired to the judge's chambers. There were some preliminary matters to be disposed of, and it was necessary that they not be heard by the jury. Uppermost in Hart's mind was the court's ruling on Wilton's motion for summary judgment. During the week he had given the matter some additional thought, and found himself even more convinced than before that the court's ruling was in error. Hart opened the proceeding with an appeal to Judge Shannon that he reverse himself and allow the payment issue to be tried. First he discussed the evidence, and then the leading Colorado Supreme Court cases on the issue of payment. Finally, he made the following argument:

> I would like to call the Court's attention to the following testimony from our deposition of Dr. Graham, defendant's father:
>
> Q: (By Mr. Hart) You heard your daughter's testimony concerning the fact that whenever she and Anne traveled in Paula's car that Anne would pay half of the expenses? Did you have any knowledge of that kind of arrangement?
> A: (Dr. Graham) Yes, generally.
> Q: You did understand that they had that kind of working arrangement?
> A: Yes.
> Q: And also that —
> A: Well, I would hardly call it a working arrangement.
> Q: To the extent that your daughter testified?
> A: A friendly arrangement.
> Q: It is probably a matter of semantics. Your daughter testified that this was a customary and usual thing for them and you did have knowledge of that fact.
> A: Yes.

Q: And on the contrary, if your daughter went with Anne it worked in reverse that your daughter contributed half of the expenses of the transportation?

A: Yes. I really think at that age they will do anything they can to raise a dollar for gasoline.

All I am trying to raise in the Court's mind is the fact that we should be permitted to present testimony into evidence as to this statement of Dr. Graham, to see if we cannot establish facts that would indicate, or facts from which the jury could reasonably infer the idea, the promise of payment that they agreed to, both depositions of the girls indicate they understood that there was this agreement. So the expectation of the payment we should be able to argue has raised a reasonable inference of a material compensation or an inducement for the trip.

More than that, and I think most sufficiently, is this. I cannot see, since this case must be tried in any event, and must go to the jury on the willful and wanton issue ... I don't see how the defendant can be prejudiced by the Court rescinding its ruling on the motion for summary judgment and permitting us to go into the details of this, and then at the conclusion of the case if the Court is of the opinion that as a matter of law the plaintiff was a guest, the Court can simply direct the jury that the plaintiff was a guest. At least this gives us an opportunity to develop this line of inquiry. Why should the Court make this precipitous ruling now that would prevent us from developing this line of inquiry when you can protect the defendant, if the defendant needs protection, as a matter of determination as a matter of law at the conclusion of the evidence.

After extensive discussion, Judge Shannon made the following statement:

Of course, part of his argument is precluding him from exploring further, for example, may it or may it not be developed, for example, that Paula Graham, the driver, had an allowance, whether she had the kind of money, this was an inducing factor that on any given weekend that she would be of assistance, and so forth and so on.

I think I had better leave the factual situation to the jury.

At this time the Court will grant a new trial on the summary judgment that was signed just this morning prior to argument, but which was ordered prepared under the pretrial order of the Court, as a result of pretrial conference. The effect then of this is that the matter or the issue of guest or non-guest is an issue to be tried.

The remaining matters were of lesser import. For example, Hart wanted permission to call a particular medical witness out of order, to accommodate the physician's schedule. Wilton wanted a clarification of the court's ruling on the seatbelt issue.

After this discussion, the attorneys and the court reporter returned to the courtroom. A moment later the judge entered, the bailiff called "all rise," and then "the District Court in and for the County of Larimer is now in session, the Honorable Judge Shannon presiding. You may be seated."

The judge called the case, ceremoniously asked each counsel if he was ready, and the formal drama began.

1. SELECTING THE JURY

The first step was the selection of the jury.

The clerk seated fourteen prospective jurors in the jury box. As a group, they were sworn to tell the truth. Then began the curious process of selecting the jury. Hart had demanded a jury of six members — the usual number, though the historic jury of twelve is still occasionally used. The six members would be chosen from the beginning panel by a process of elimination. Each side is allowed to indicate that it does not want a certain number of the beginning panel; any juror so indicated is excused from service. In Colorado, each side is allowed to dismiss four potential jurors. This dismissal is called a "peremptory challenge." Accordingly, to get a panel of six jurors, the clerk must start with at least fourteen potential jurors. Under this system, the jury that remains might be viewed as the middle six of the original fourteen. The defendant will have struck the four she perceived as most pro-plaintiff, and the plaintiff will have struck the four she perceived as most pro-defendant. Some believe that the net result is a more homogenous and less interesting group than would be true without peremptory challenges.

In addition to peremptory challenges, a juror may be challenged "for cause." Cause would include anything that might impair the juror's ability, open-mindedness, or impartiality. For example, if the juror is a close relative of one of the parties, or a close friend who admits that such close friendship would make it difficult to be impartial, then the court would dismiss the juror, an additional prospective juror would be added to the panel in the dismissed juror's place, and neither party would use up a peremptory challenge.

After the jurors are sworn to tell the truth, the attorneys and the judge may question each juror. The process of questioning the jurors is referred to as *voir dire*. If a juror is found to be biased or is otherwise disqualified on *voir dire*, that juror is challenged for cause and excused. Another potential juror then is called, sworn, and seated. After all jurors have been questioned, the attorneys may each exercise their peremptory challenges. This is done in turn; first, one by plaintiff; next, one by defendant; then a second by plaintiff, and so on.

The lawyer's right to reject, for any or no reason, any four jurors gives rise to one of the most interesting problems in law practice: How can one tell which potential jurors will help one's case and which will hurt it? If the wrong juror is left on the panel, that juror may persuade the other five that one's opponent ought to prevail. The peremptory challenge, then, is important if one can exercise it effectively. In order to exercise the challenges effectively, the lawyer is given a fairly broad scope in questioning the potential juror. But what questions will help you make that decision? It always seems important to have some general personal information about the juror: age, occupation, marital status, spouse's occupation, number of children and their ages, etc. Some lawyers try to obtain, in advance of trial, the religious and ethnic backgrounds of the potential jurors and their approximate income. In addition, the simple process of asking the potential jurors any questions at all will give the attorney some idea of how the juror's mind works. Finally, the lawyer can try to draw from the potential jurors their reactions to the type of case involved. It might be useful for both Hart and Wilton to know, for example, that a potential juror finds driving in snow very difficult, or thinks adolescents should not be so concerned about their appearance, or thinks automobile insurance rates are already much too high.

Specific information of this type is very useful, but jurors do not often provide the lawyer with such obvious tags. The use that can be made of the more general personal information is more questionable. There is considerable folklore in the profession about how to identify defendant-oriented and plaintiff-oriented jurors. According to that folklore, for example, people of Mediterranean extraction, Jews, Catholics, and young adults are more likely to be influenced by sympathy, which in turn means they will be more likely to allow recovery where the liability is doubtful and will award larger amounts for damages. Likewise, the very poor and the very rich are thought to be more likely to bring in very large verdicts. On the other hand, engineers, civil servants, and science professors are supposed to be stingy, but school teachers and liberal arts professors are supposed to be generous. A juror who has ethnic, professional, or other characteristics in common with your client is presumed to be more likely to be well-disposed towards your client.

What factors would you rely upon? Some experienced attorneys believe that there is no way to tell in advance which potential jurors will be favorable or unfavorable. But the predominant view is that careful selection makes a substantial difference. In fact, in large cases attorneys will go to great lengths in planning the use of their peremptory challenges. At the most extreme, some law firms "pre-try" particularly large cases to different groups of mock jurors, using professional psychologists to develop profiles of mock jurors who responded favorably and unfavorably.[10] The attorneys obtain the list of persons in the jury

---

[10] The psychologist will also use this opportunity to determine which aspects of the attorneys' presentations were most effective in persuading the mock jurors and which aspects were offensive or least effective. The attorneys will use this information to plan their presentation of the case.

pool for the particular case as early as possible, and use investigators to learn about each person on the list. This information is used to plan *voir dire*. Finally, the attorney will huddle with the psychologist (who has been observing the potential jurors during *voir dire*) to determine which jurors to challenge. (The investigator and the psychologist are also very helpful in developing challenges for cause, which, if successful, effectively add to the attorney's control over the composition of the jury.)

Needless to say, all of this is very, very expensive, though also probably very effective. The effectiveness of these expensive aids raises troubling questions about the increasing cost of obtaining a fair trial, particularly in cases in which only one side can afford this type of help.

Although *voir dire* is ostensibly only for the purpose of examining each potential juror's suitability, in fact attorneys use *voir dire* for many other purposes. Many will use *voir dire* to start planting their theory of the case, or to develop sympathy for their clients. *Voir dire* is also an opportunity to establish rapport with the jurors; the questioning can be considerably less formal than the rest of the trial, and it is the attorneys' only opportunity for give and take with the jurors. If the jurors develop a preference for one of the attorneys, or decide that they trust one attorney more than the other, they will be much more likely to accept that attorney's view of the case.

Many lawyers hold the view that the opportunity for abuse presented by the free use of *voir dire* examination is not justified by the information it yields. This view has led to a practice, followed in federal courts, in which the judge rather than the attorneys conducts the *voir dire* examination. The attorneys may submit questions to the judge to be asked of the potential jurors, but the judge is not required to ask them. In most state courts, however, questioning on *voir dire* remains primarily with the lawyer.

In our case, each attorney used all four challenges. Hart's peremptory challenges included the manager of the local airport and a member of the campus police. Wilton's challenges went to the younger members of the panel. Can you guess at the reasons for their respective choices?

After the jury was selected, the jurors took a second oath, this one to "well and truly try the matter at issue ..., and a true verdict render, according to the evidence."

2. OPENING STATEMENTS

Prior to the presentation of the evidence, each attorney has an opportunity to make an opening statement to the jury. Though the jury has been given some glimpse of the case in *voir dire*, the opening statement is the attorney's first opportunity to make an organized presentation of the case. In the opening statement the lawyer explains what she hopes to prove and how she hopes to prove it. She will not be able to talk directly to the jury again until after all the evidence has been presented, so it is important the that attorney impress upon them, in terms they will understand and remember, just what it is she is trying to accomplish.

a. Plaintiff's Opening Statement

The plaintiff's opening statement comes first. In our case, Hart began as follows:

> THE COURT: The plaintiff may make their opening statement to the jury.
> MR. HART: Ladies and gentlemen of the jury:
> This is an opening statement made on behalf of the plaintiff in this case, Anne Rasmussen.
> What I have to say to you, as the Court will instruct you, or perhaps already has, is not to be considered by you as evidence. Nor when Mr. Wilton makes his opening statement; his remarks do not constitute evidence in this case.
> The purpose of an opening statement is to permit the attorneys for the parties to describe to you what they intend, expect, or hope that the evidence and testimony will show. I intend to review what I anticipate will come from the testimony and evidence and to orient the jury as to the total picture of what we intend and hope to present to you in the form of testimony and evidence. Because it is going to come to you in the trial in bits and pieces. It is going to come to you through various documents or photographs that will be presented.
> I like to consider an opening statement to a jury as somewhat like a promissory note. I don't want to promise to you something that cannot be delivered. I don't want to exaggerate what the testimony and evidence is going to show. I must tell you that sometimes there are surprises in a trial. Sometimes we think we can get in some evidence that the Court tells us should not be permitted to go to the jury. And so it doesn't go to the jury. But within that limitation I believe that the facts that I am going to recite for you will be demonstrated and shown to you by the testimony and evidence in this case.
> The testimony and evidence in this case will demonstrate that the two parties in this case, the plaintiff, Anne Rasmussen, and the defendant, Paula Graham, were both 17 years of age at the time the collision in this case occurred, which was on December 30, 1980. They had known each other for, I think, about a year. And they were good friends.

And so he continued, discussing, step by step, in detail, what testimony he expected from each witness. As you remember, Hart had three factual issues to develop:

1. Anne was a passenger for "payment";
2. Paula was negligent and her negligence was "willful and wanton"; and
3. The amount of Anne's injuries.

In his opening statement, Hart outlined these three issues, and then explained to the jury how he hoped to prove each. He described, in great detail, the evidence he would present. He concluded by reminding the jury that

> what I have told you I remind you again is not evidence. I have tried to recite to you what I think the evidence and testimony will show to you. But what I have said to you is not evidence and the same thing can be said concerning the opening statement that Mr. Wilton will now make.

b. Defendant's Opening Statement

Wilton, of course, had the same three issues, but for him, the job was reversed. He had to show that Anne was not a passenger for payment, and that Paula was not negligent, or at least not willful and wanton. Wilton had made, in advance of trial, a tactical decision concerning the damages issue: He had decided that his case more or less depended on the guest statute, and he felt confident that he could prevail on that issue. As a theoretical matter, the extent of Anne's damages was unrelated to the payment issue, and Wilton was certainly free to argue both "no payment" and "no (or little) damages." Anne had obviously been seriously injured, however, and Wilton was afraid that his efforts to minimize her damages might offend the jury sufficiently to prejudice him on the payment issue. After all, the jurors were human, and if they were sufficiently offended by the defendant's tactics on one issue, they might well lean towards the plaintiff on all the issues. So, in his opening statement, Wilton concentrated on the guest issue, spent some time on the negligence issues, and said very little about damages.

Wilton concluded as follows:

> Ladies and gentlemen of the jury, although what I have told you is not proof, it is the proof that we believe will be presented at the time of this trial and we believe that the proof that we will be basically showing you is not that an accident did not happen — it did — and not that injuries did not occur from this accident. They did. But rather we will be offering proof regarding the responsibility and the manner, if you wish, in which this accident happened. And also we will examine in detail the relationship between these two girls. Were they friends or were there other purposes motivating them to go on this trip, other than a purely social friendship? We believe the evidence will show that it was a friendship and their relationship and that the general accident happened, and lest we be construed at any other time, we believe the evidence will show and we will elicit questions to this effect that, ladies and gentlemen of the jury, nobody is sorrier that this accident

happened and that there were damages in fact, than the defendant Paula Graham and her father.

MR. HART: I ask the Court to ask the jury to disregard that. But I hate to do that in an opening statement. But it is not a matter subject to proof. Everybody is sorry.

THE COURT: Sustained. It is not a part of the case. You are instructed to disregard the matter.

MR. WILTON: Ladies and gentlemen of the jury, I thank you for your attention to our side and hope that you will, as indicated before, you will listen to all of the evidence and wait until all of the evidence is in before you make your decision in this case.

QUESTION

What was objectionable about Wilton's statement?

3. PRESENTATION OF THE EVIDENCE

a. An Overview

The plaintiff (i.e., the person who commenced the case) is usually the person asking the court to change the status quo, either by awarding damages, entering an injunction, or granting other relief. Because there is an inherent reluctance to act, at least until the reasons for acting are clear, the burden is on the plaintiff to convince the court that it should act, not on the defendant to convince the court that it should not act. In simpler terms, ties go to the defendant: if neither side persuades the court, matters are left as they were, which is a victory for the defendant.

It follows that the plaintiff must present her case first. She must show why the court should act, before the defendant will be required to show why it should not. When plaintiff has finished presenting her case, (i.e., when plaintiff "rests her case"), the court will then have to decide if she presented enough evidence to permit a jury to decide in her favor. If she did not, then there is no reason to go further: she had her chance to convince the court; she did not introduce enough evidence to convince the court; matters should be left as they were.

Defendant will raise this issue by making a motion for directed verdict or a motion for judgment as a matter of law. Defendant will argue that even if plaintiff's evidence is viewed in its most favorable light, it is not enough to convince a reasonable person that plaintiff's view of the facts should prevail; if the jury were to return a verdict for plaintiff on this weak evidence, it would mean that the jury either ignored the evidence or ignored the instructions, acting instead out of confusion or sympathy. If the judge believes that the evidence for plaintiff is so slight that the jury could not follow the instructions and still find for plaintiff, then she will grant defendant's directed verdict motion, and the case will be dismissed.

If, as is usual, defendant's directed verdict motion is denied, defendant then gets to present her "case in chief." At the close of defendant's case, plaintiff may move for directed verdict at the close of defendant's case. In contrast with defendant's motion, plaintiff's motion will seldom be appropriate. This is because plaintiff carries the burden of persuading the jury; even if she presents substantial evidence and the defendant presents no evidence, the jury might not be persuaded by plaintiff's evidence; if it is not persuaded, plaintiff loses. Thus, even though plaintiff's evidence seems to the judge much more persuasive than defendant's, usually she must deny plaintiff's motion and leave the case for the jury's decision. Despite the disparity in the evidence, the jury might follow the instructions and still find for the defendant because it was still unpersuaded either way.

Occasionally plaintiff's case will be so strong that the judge will rule that the jury has to be persuaded by it unless defendant adequately rebuts. One common example would be an action on a promissory note in which plaintiff presents the note with defendant's signature and testimony that the signature is in fact defendant's. If defendant did not rebut this testimony or raise an adequate affirmative defense (such as statute of limitations or fraud in the inducement), the jury would be not be permitted to disbelieve plaintiff's case, and plaintiff's motion for directed verdict at the close of defendant's evidence would be granted.

After defendant rests her case and plaintiff's motion for directed verdict, if any, is denied, plaintiff is given a chance to rebut any new issues raised by defendant's evidence. In rare cases, when plaintiff's rebuttal raises significant new issues, defendant will be given a chance to rebut plaintiff's rebuttal.

In summary, plaintiff presents her case in chief. When plaintiff rests, defendant may well move for directed verdict. When defendant's motion is denied, defendant then presents her case in chief, which is followed by plaintiff's rebuttal and, occasionally, defendant's rebuttal.

At the close of all the evidence, it is common for defendants to renew their motions for directed verdict.

The attorneys then present their closing arguments. Ordinarily, plaintiff argues first, defendant responds, and plaintiff is then permitted to rebut; plaintiff will have the same amount of time as defendant, but will have the valuable right to divide her time between her initial closing argument and her rebuttal; this advantage is usually explained as a compensation for the fact that plaintiff carries the burden of proof. In most jurisdictions, the judge will read the instructions to the jury after closing arguments, and the case will then be given to the jury.

b. Eliciting Testimony

The preceding paragraphs show how the evidence begins with plaintiff's case in chief, followed by defendant's case in chief, plaintiff's rebuttal and occasionally defendant's rebuttal. Let's look a little more closely at how the testimony is actually elicited. When plaintiff presents her case, she gets to present all of her witnesses; when she has finished with her last witness, she rests her case. She may arrange her witnesses in any order, but she can only call a witness once, so she had better ask all the questions she has of that witness while the witness is on the stand.

With each of her witnesses, plaintiff gets to complete all of her questions before defendant is permitted to ask any questions.[11] This initial questioning of the party's witness is referred to as direct examination. Questioning proceeds just as it did at Anne's deposition. The witness is first sworn to tell the truth. The attorney who is offering the witness's evidence then proceeds to elicit the testimony. The witness is not asked to engage in a long narrative. The court is interested in very specific information, and the witness, if left alone, would likely include a great deal of information extraneous to the narrow issues of the case. Further, opposing counsel would have no way of anticipating objectionable statements from the witness, and therefore could not object until after the jury had heard inadmissible testimony. So the testimony proceeds through specific questions by counsel, followed by answers from the witness.

The attorney's questions must not be too general, as that would invite a narrative from the witness. But neither may the lawyer's questions be too detailed. If the attorney's question is really a long story, followed by "isn't that true," then the jury is being given the evidence in the words of the attorney, who was not an observer of the facts testified to, who was not sworn, and whose statements are likely to be given credence by the jury disproportionate to their credibility. A question that is too detailed, in the sense of suggesting its own answer, is referred to as a "leading question."

---

[11] There is a limited exception to this principle. At times a party will use her witness to establish the foundation for the admission of certain evidence; for example, the witness might testify to the authenticity of a document, or to her credentials as an expert witness. At the completion of this foundation, the party will offer the particular evidence (e.g., the document, or expert testimony from this witness) into evidence. The judge will have to evaluate the foundational testimony, in order to decide whether or not to admit the evidence. Before the judge reaches her decision, it is only fair to allow the opposing party to ask some questions of the witness regarding the foundation, so that the opponent will be able to identify a basis for opposing the admissibility of the particular evidence. When she asks these questions during the offering party's direct examination, the opposing party is said to "*voir dire*" the foundational witness, or to take the witness on "*voir dire*." This usage should not be confused with the attorneys' opportunity to *voir dire* potential jurors. After the judge rules on the admissibility of the evidence, the presenting party is permitted to continue her direct examination of the witness.

In some courts, attorneys must stand behind the lectern when they question witnesses. In most courts, attorneys are given some latitude. If the attorney wants the witness to impress the jury, she will frequently conduct her questioning from a point near the jury, so that when the witness looks at the attorney during the direct examination, the witness will also be looking at the jury. And, as an important point of etiquette, an attorney must always stand when addressing a witness or the judge in open court.

During the course of questioning the opposing attorney must listen closely for objectionable questions. If she fails to object before the witness answers the question, the objection will be waived unless earlier objection was not feasible. The lawyer stands and briefly states the nature of her objection; Hart's objection during Wilton's opening statement is a typical example. Other examples would be "Your Honor, that question calls for hearsay" or "Objection, your Honor, that question has already been asked and answered."

Ordinarily the judge will look to the opposing attorney for a brief response. The response must be made to the judge; opposing attorneys never address each other in open court. If the attorney feels she needs more than a few words, or that her response should not be heard by the jury, she will ask permission to approach the bench for what is known as a conference "at sidebar." At times, when extended argument is necessary or when further questions of the witness are necessary to rule on the objection, the jury will be excused.

After plaintiff finishes direct examination of her witness, defendant will conduct cross examination. Usually the witness will be adverse to the cross examiner. The cross examiner may "lead the witness" through the use of "leading questions" (questions which suggest the answer). Such questions, frequently in the form of "Isn't it true that ..." are simply an attempt to put words in the mouth of the witness. This is appropriate, because a witness will not allow an adverse attorney to put words in her mouth unless they are strictly accurate, whereas she might be more willing to accept inaccurate or imprecise descriptions suggested by an attorney who is on her side.

After defendant completes cross examination, plaintiff may be allowed to ask a few additional questions of her witness, as "redirect" examination. Redirect will be limited to new information brought out curing cross examination.

The process is exactly the same when defendant is presenting her witnesses, though the parties are reversed. Defendant conducts direct examination of the witness, plaintiff cross examines, and defendant redirects.

i. Plaintiff's case in chief

Hart's witnesses included:

1. Three observers of the actual collision: Anne, Paula, and the driver of the pickup truck that was coming from the other direction.

2. Another witness with considerable information about the accident, even though he had not actually seen it: the State Patrolman who was called to the scene.

3. Three witnesses who had information about the payment issue: Anne, Paula, and Dr. Graham.

4. A number of witnesses who had information about Anne's damages: Anne, Paula, the driver of the pickup truck who saw her immediately after the accident, the surgeon who treated Anne, Anne's parents, and the music director at Colorado State University, who would testify to the flute scholarship that Anne would have been able to accept had she not sustained certain injuries to the nerves in her upper lip.

In what order should these witnesses be called to testify? It might be logical to call them to testify on each of the factual issues in turn. Under this arrangement, the witnesses who would testify on the issue of negligence might be called first; "payment" witnesses second; and damages witnesses third. But one witness will testify about two of these issues (the driver of the pickup) and two witnesses will testify about all three (Paula and Anne). Because Hart can call each witness only once, he will have to elicit testimony on two issues when he examines the pick-up driver, and on all three issues when he examines Anne and (if he chooses to call her as his witness) Paula. So, organizing his presentation by issue was not feasible for Hart.

(a) Examination of the patrolman

(1) Direct examination

It is customary to call the plaintiff as the first witness. In this case, however, that would have required starting proof on all three issues, each of which would then have had to be explored separately with subsequent witnesses. Furthermore, Hart had found in his discussions with the patrolman that the latter would be a favorable witness for his case. Calling him first, then, would start the case off with a discussion of the accident only and would help keep the issues simple. It would also give the jurors a favorable statement from a witness who was, and would be perceived as being, impartial. So plaintiff's first witness was the patrolman.

After he was sworn, Hart first took the patrolman over his qualifications as a witness. These included his very thorough familiarity with the area in which the accident occurred, his actual observation of the vehicles shortly after the accident, and his formal training and experience in evaluating the cause of automobile accidents. In other words, the patrolman was qualified both as an observer of certain pertinent real-world facts and as an expert who could provide the jury with help in drawing inferences from those facts.

Hart's direct examination of the patrolman concerned a number of matters. First, Hart took the witness through a detailed description of the scene of the accident as it appeared when he arrived there. This included the introduction into evidence of certain photographs he had taken, as well as certain measurements (such as the width of the road and the length of the skidmarks).

Next Hart examined the witness on the question of the point at which the snowplow would have first been visible to Paula. This was a matter of great importance, as the farther away the snowplow was when Paula could first have seen it, the greater her negligence in not stopping the Tercel before hitting it. Prior to trial, Hart had asked the witness to go back to the scene and determine at what point an object of the size of the snowplow could have first been seen from a Tercel. He had done that, and at the trial testified that this distance was four-tenths of a mile.

Finally, Hart examined the witness as follows:

Q: (by Hart): Now, sir, in the area immediately west of the scene of the accident, where the road enters the canyon, will you describe for the jury the road condition as you entered that canyon and proceeded to the scene of the collision on December 30, 1980?

A: It was generally snowpacked with a few bare spots here and there, mostly just where the Highway Department had sanded with coal slack, generally speaking this was on the hills that they had done this.

Q: Sir, you indicated earlier in your examination you had driven this road so many times that you couldn't estimate it. Was that in both winter and summer?

A: Yes, sir.

Q. And you have also testified you drove the road from the west in the vicinity of Craig to the scene of the collision?

A: Yes, sir.

Q: What is in your opinion the maximum safe speed in that area?

MR. WILTON: Your Honor, I am going to object unless more foundation is laid, referring particularly to whether it is this accident or another accident or what he is talking about in terms of road conditions and all the other factors involved here.

MR. HART: Well, Your Honor, I am simply asking the Officer if he has an opinion as to the reasonably safe maximum speed. His training and education I think are adequate that the Court can find and other Courts have found, that he is able to.

THE COURT: This is on the date in question, the date of the accident?

MR. HART: Yes.

THE COURT: He may give his opinion.

Q: Now, sir, I don't want any misunderstanding. I want you to testify as to what your opinion is of the maximum reasonable safe speed that a vehicle traveling in the area, in the area this Tercel was traveling, on the day of the collision, could have been driven in that area on that day?

A: Yes, sir. Forty miles an hour, sir.

Q: Sir, so there will be no misunderstanding relative to your opinion concerning the maximum reasonable safe speed, will you describe to the jury the area in which you are testifying relative to that speed.

A: I would be referring to the entire canyon area, but specifically to the area of the accident.

(2) Cross examination

Cross examination gives the opposing counsel the opportunity to challenge the reliability of the evidence. The cross examiner will try to discredit or impeach the testimony of the witness. There are a number of ways this can be done. The cross examiner might be able to show that the witness has either a reason or a tendency to distort, such as a bias in favor or against one of the parties or an interest in the result. By asking about other details of the occurrence, the cross examination might show the witness's memory of the circumstances to which he testified is not as complete as might have been inferred from the witness's direct testimony. It might show that the witness was not in a position actually to observe all that was testified to on direct. The cross examination might show behavior or prior statements of the witness that indicate the witness did not really believe the story she told in court.

The patrolman's testimony that forty miles per hour was the maximum safe speed was very damaging to Paula's case. Even Paula was going to admit that she was going forty-five miles per hour, and the other two observers of the accident were going to put her speed higher — between fifty and sixty miles per hour.

The following is an excerpt from Wilton's cross examination of this witness:

Q: You testified that you were in the Craig, Colorado, vicinity at the time that you received the call?

A: Yes, sir.

Q: How far is Craig from the scene of this accident?

A: Twenty-seven miles, sir.

Q: And you received the call at 11:36, approximately?

A: Yes.

Q: And you arrived at the scene at 12:01?

A: Yes, sir.

Q: Do you know how fast you drove to get there from where you were?

A: No, sir.

Q: Was it more than 40 miles an hour?

A: Yes, sir.

Q: And were you driving safely?
A: Yes, sir.

Wilton also questioned the witness as follows about his testimony regarding visibility:

Q: You testified that when you determined that the scene of the accident was visible from a point four-tenths of a mile, you were in your vehicle, as I understand it?
A: Yes, sir.
Q: And that in your vehicle you came up from the west going east on this road and looked down the road to see the first point at which you could see the scene of the accident. Is that correct?
A: Right.
Q: Now, first of all, what kind of a car did you have?
A: 1993 Chevrolet.
Q: Is this a Colorado State Vehicle?
A: Yes, sir.
Q: Is it the same size as the Tercel?
A: No, sir.
Q: Is it higher or lower?
A: Higher.
Q: Well, Officer, wouldn't it possibly permit, if you were elevated higher, permit you to see a little further?
A: Yes, sir.

QUESTIONS

1. Is this cross examination effective? How would you, as a juror, react to it?
2. Could Wilton have made his cross examination on the issue of the maximum safe speed more effective? Should he simply have left this issue alone?

(3) Redirect examination

After Wilton completed his cross examination, Hart was allowed to attempt to rehabilitate his witness. As with the cross examination, redirect examination is not supposed to open any new matter, but is to be directed only towards undoing any damage from the opposing attorney's examination.

The following is an excerpt from Hart's redirect examination:

Q: Officer, you were asked how you drove to the scene of this collision. Would you state whether or not you had your red light on, warning light on?
A: No, sir, I did not.
Q: Did you use the siren?
A: No, sir.

Q: Will you describe how you drove to the scene of the collision after you entered the canyon?

A: How do you mean?

Q: Speed and manner that you drove?

A: I can't recollect the exact speed. Of course, I know this road as well as most people know their own backyard. I know exactly how fast I can stay in any curve there under almost any condition, make my living this way. This is my business.

Q: When you say you drove 60 miles per hour, that doesn't mean you drove at 60 miles per hour all the way?

A: I don't recollect saying I drove 60 miles an hour. Did I? I don't recollect naming that speed.

Q: I thought that you did. Officer, the fact that there is a speed limit sign that says 60 miles an hour as you enter the canyon, does that indicate to you as a patrolman and law officer that a person can lawfully drive 60 miles an hour in that canyon regardless of the condition of the road?

A: No, sir.

Q: Why is that, sir?

A: Colorado law requires that a person adjust their speed to the adjusting conditions, whatever they may be.

Q: And you, sir, were of the opinion that the maximum safe speed in that area was 40 miles per hour?

A: Yes, sir.

Within the discretion of the judge, the opponent of the evidence can follow the redirect examination with recross examination, and so on, but that is seldom necessary. Wilton did not recross examine the patrolman, and after redirect the witness was excused.

(b) Examination of the driver of the pickup truck

(1) Direct examination

Hart's next witness was the driver of the pickup truck. He testified that he was traveling west on Highway 40 at the time and place of the accident. He testified that he saw the snowplow and that he saw the Tercel come into view. He estimated (over Wilton's vigorous objection) that the Tercel was traveling between fifty and sixty miles per hour. He testified that when he saw it, he realized that it was going to have trouble stopping in time, although it was "quite a way in back of the snowplow." He was nearly alongside the snowplow when the Tercel hit it. After the accident he pulled off the road and went to help. He was able to describe, in gruesome detail, the scene immediately after the accident.

(2) Cross examination

On cross, Wilton brought out the fact that the pickup driver did not know exactly how fast his own vehicle was going at the time he estimated the Tercel's speed. He also brought out that the witness could not remember where the Tercel was when it first came into his view. On direct, the witness had testified that immediately after the accident, he had gone down the road to the west to flag down traffic. Wilton's cross examination on this point was as follows:

Q: Finally, after the accident occurred, you said you walked down the road to the west of the accident.

A: Yes.

Q: You were concerned that other traffic might come upon this scene and not know what had happened?

A: The road was in such a condition that they couldn't stop if they got very close and the traffic was very fast.

Q: You were afraid, if I understand your testimony then, that they could not see this in sufficient time to come to a stop.

A: Yes.

Q: And that is because there was a crest of a hill just shortly to the west of the accident.

A: Just a small crest. I walked up just as far, or far enough to see good and see the oncoming traffic.

Q: And this is the reason that you took it upon yourself to do this because you were concerned another vehicle might not see the scene and know what had happened and you wanted to slow them?

A: Yes.

Q: Now, you have heard the officer testify that he had full vision at a distance of four-tenths of a mile.

A: Yes.

Q: Did you walk four-tenths of a mile?

A: No. Just far enough to get up where I could stop the traffic.

Q: How far was that?

A: Not very far.

Q: Could you estimate the distance for us.

A: Oh, I would say maybe a hundred, two hundred yards.

Q: Thank you, I have no further questions.

(c) Examination of plaintiff

To this point, Hart had given the jury a favorable but not unblemished picture of the way in which the accident occurred. This picture had come from disinterested witnesses. Hart had prepared the ground for Anne's testimony, and she was called as the next witness.

(1) Direct examination

Hart wanted to develop three separate issues with Anne: the accident, "payment," and her injuries. Ideally, he would develop her testimony regarding the accident first, as the jury was already focused on this issue. However, as a chronological matter, the facts concerning payment preceded the facts of the accident. Furthermore, the testimony about the preceding facts would be easier for Anne to talk about than the facts of the accident, and that might give Anne and the jury a chance to get used to each other before the more critical testimony was reached.

After developing some background personal information, Hart questioned Anne about the events leading up to the trip to Steamboat Springs, and then up to the trip to Craig.

At that point he elicited testimony concerning "payment":

Q: Had you and Paula Graham ever had any discussion concerning the payment of the expenses when, for example, you were riding as a passenger in her car?

A: Yes.

Q: Did you have discussions with her or a discussion concerning payment of expenses when she was riding with you in a car that you had obtained?

A: Yes, except for that my car was owned by my father and I didn't drive all the time. My father used his credit card. It was usually full.

Q: What was the nature of the discussions or discussion that you had with Paula Graham concerning expenses of transportation when you rode as a passenger in her automobile?

A: I always paid for half of the gas.

Q: Did you discuss this with her, this payment?

A: Are you talking about this time?

Q: Prior to this time.

A: We always discussed it. It was like understood.

Hart then elicited testimony regarding the arrangements for this trip.

Next, Hart explored, in detail, the events immediately preceding the accident. This included Anne's testimony that she had observed the speedometer just before they saw the snowplow, and it indicated that the Tercel was going 60 miles per hour.

Her testimony regarding the accident was as follows:

Q: As you approached this snowplow could you tell approximately, if you can, how far away from the snowplow you were when you first saw it?

A: It was a long ways away and we saw it a long time before we hit it. I can't say in seconds or anything. But I would say two or three city blocks, like in downtown Fort Collins.

Q: When you saw the snowplow and the blue pickup? Was there any conversation between you and Paula Graham?

A: When we saw them?

Q: Yes.

A: Just sort of looked at her and she looked at me and we were going really fast. And I don't know if we said anything out loud. But I braced myself. I held onto the front of the car. It was very obvious that we weren't going to make it, you know. We weren't going to stop or else we weren't going to be able to pass the snowplow on the left because the truck was coming the other way.

Hart also elicited the following testimony:

Q: All right. After this collision on December 30, 1994, did you ever after that have a conversation with Paula Graham concerning the occurrence of this collision?

A: Yes, I did.

Q: Where was that discussion?

A: In the hospital a few days after the accident.

Q: And that was in Denver?

A: Yes.

Q: And did Paula Graham say anything to you relative to the facts now concerning her driving immediately prior to the collision?

A: She told me that she was speeding, there was no question about that, and that she was going 60 around the curve to the left

Q: Did you ever have a conversation with her after that time of the conversation in the hospital in Denver?

A: Yes, I did.

Q: And was this conversation concerning the speed with which she had been driving just prior to the collision?

A: Yes.

Q: And where was that conversation?

A: In my home.

Q: And about when?

A: It was probably a few weeks after I got out of the hospital.

Q: How did you happen to be talking to her at that time concerning this matter? I mean in what way were you talking to her?

A: She called me on the telephone.

Q: And did she make any comment or statement to you then concerning the speed with which she was driving just prior to the collision?

A: Yes, she did.

Q: Was that statement the same or different than the statement she had made to you when she talked to you about it in the hospital?

A: Different.

Q: And in what way was it different?

A: Well, she told me, she asked me what my story was. She said, well, maybe, you know, she wasn't sure what she told me before, that maybe she was going 40. Now, you know, never know. She wanted to know what I said.

Following the discussion of the accident, Hart explored the nature of the injuries she had sustained. Hart asked a number of questions, requiring detailed answers about her impact with the dashboard, her physical sensations at the time of the accident and at times thereafter, the treatment — surgical, medical, and dental — which she had received and was still receiving, and her continuing disabilities, discomfort, and embarrassment. Anne's answers were detailed, forcing the jurors to visualize the injuries in a fairly vivid sense. It was an upsetting process for Anne, as well as for the others in the courtroom, and it was on this note that Hart finished his direct examination.

(2) Cross examination

Wilton was obliged to start his cross examination, in a very gentle tone, with the following statement.

Q: Miss Rasmussen, I hope you understand that if you don't understand any of my questions, or if you feel that if you want me to stop asking you questions so that you can compose yourself, that you will ask me at any time. Do you understand?

A: Yes.

Wilton, too, began his examination of Anne with an exploration of the general background that preceded the trip. He was anxious to get across to the jury the message that Paula and Anne had been good friends, and that Paula's invitation had nothing to do with "payment."

After spending some time on this issue, Wilton turned to the accident itself. Wilton cross examined her as follows:

Q: Now, when did you say that you first recalled having seen the snowplow?

A: I said two to three city blocks.... What do you mean by that question?

Q: All right. I will hand you what has been marked previously as Plaintiff's Exhibit B, which is a diagram of the road at the point at which the accident occurred. Now on this exhibit, can you indicate where it was that you recall that you first saw the snowplow ahead of you? And perhaps if I have a marking pencil, you may mark it with an X.

A: It was back in here [indicating].

Q: Excuse me. Now, I am sorry I didn't hear what you said.

A: Back in here [indicating].

Q: Is it right where you have placed an *X*, with a circle around it?

A: I can't tell the exact place. That is the region where it was.

Q: Could it have been farther to the east than that?

A: To the east?

Q: Yes, down the incline toward the point where the accident occurred?

A: No.

Q: Miss Rasmussen, I refer you to line 23 of your deposition that you gave under oath in April and ask you to look —

MR. HART: What page?

MR. WILTON: Page 23.

Q: Starting with line 18 will you read that?

A: Out loud?

Q: No.... You have read it now, have you?

A: Yes.

Q: Now I am going to ask you again does this refresh your recollection as to where you first saw this snow grader?

A: The problem with this is that — well, this says the truth. But when you took this deposition, like you really didn't know. Everybody was in so much of a mix about the curves. I am talking about the curve on the left. And when we came off that down there, when we saw it, we were on an incline. I said that here.

Q: So you were coming down the incline?

A: Well, let me see. When we were coming out of the curve.

Q: And then the question was you were coming down an incline? Is that what I understand?

A: I don't know if we were on the incline yet. But right as we came out of the curve.

Q: Well, I am not really trying to confuse you. I want to know what your testimony is, where you saw it, on top of the hill where you indicated there was a mark on the photograph, or whether it was actually coming down the hill on the incline when you first saw the snowplow?

A: Well, as you keep telling it, it went so fast by the time I saw it, we saw it there we would be going down the incline. Do you know what I mean?

Q: I understand it. Now, you have indicated that you thought that you were two to three city blocks away?

A: Yes.

Q: Would you please turn to page 24 of the deposition. And if you would start with line 9 where I have asked the question, "Can you say how far ahead of your car the snowplow was when you first saw the snowplow?"

A: Yes.

Q: Could you please read the next few lines to yourself.

A: I understand.

Q: Have you read those lines?

A: Yes.

Q: Was your answer at that time that you were one city block away when you first saw the snowplow?

A: Yes, but can I explain that?

Q: We were estimating distances at that time?

A: Yes.

Q: Your estimate at that time was that it was a city block and I asked you what you meant by one city block?

A: Yes.

Q: We then talked about a downtown Fort Collins city block?

A: Yes. You wanted me to say a distance and I told you I couldn't. And since I took this, after you talked about this I went downtown and looked. I had no idea how long a city block was. Because I wanted to be correct. And I didn't know at the time sitting in the office.

Q: These are all estimates?

A: Yes.[12]

Q: All right. So at that time you said you thought it was a city block and now you think it was some further distance?

A: I had the same distance in my head but I had no idea how big a city block was.[13]

Q: Okay. Now, at the time when you first saw the snowplow, do you recall what Paula did?

A: I don't know what she did. What do you mean by that?

Q: Didn't you testify you thought maybe she came over a bit as to pass?

A: When we first saw it. It was so far away she wouldn't have gone in the other lane then. We looked at each other and we knew we saw the snowplow. There was another car coming and pretty likely that we were going to run into it.

Q: You felt like you would?

A: We must have gone quite a few feet to think about these things. But yes, we were going really fast and that is why we hit it.

---

[12] One city block would be approximately 350 feet. Two to three city blocks would be approximately 700 to 1000 feet. And .4 mile (the patrolman's estimate) is approximately 2100 feet.

[13] Note Wilton's use of the deposition as a means of impeaching Anne's testimony. This impeachment will not only cast some doubt on her statement that she saw the snowplow when the Tercel was two to three city blocks from it, but will also allow Wilton to argue that the rest of her in-court testimony might have been similarly exaggerated. Reread the pertinent portion of Wilton's cross examination. You can see how he was thinking of this cross examination at the very time he was questioning Anne at the deposition. Note also that he has gotten Anne to testify in "city blocks" at the trial, which makes it easier for him to impeach her with her deposition testimony.

Q: Do you remember that I asked you if you knew how fast the car was going just before the collision occurred? Do you remember my asking that question? As the car came over the hill, just before you saw the snowplow. Do you know how fast the car was going at that time?

A: No. But I didn't notice any reducing of speed, and I knew we were going over sixty just before that.

Q: Now as a matter of fact, what you are telling us now is that you didn't notice any decrease in speed. Is that correct?

A: Yes.

Q: If I understand your testimony, you do not know how fast the car was going at that point in time?

A: Not exactly.

Q: Now, you have testified that you saw this car, the snowplow that you considered to be a long way away?

A: Yes.

Q: You now testify you think — well, it is not one city block, you now think it is two or three city blocks?

A: Yes.

Q: Miss Rasmussen, did you say anything to Paula when you first saw that snowplow, between the time you first saw the snowplow and the time the accident occurred?

A: I don't remember any words that were said between us. We looked at each other and we acknowledged it.

Q: But you didn't have any conversation after the time that you saw the snowplow?

A: Correct.

Q: All right. What did you do as you were sitting there in the car as the car was approaching the snowplow? You weren't talking? You first said you looked at each other.

A: Then, I looked at the road and was holding on.

Q: If you will turn to page 27 of your deposition, on the last line of that page. If you would start with line 22 and read that to yourself down through line 25, and then the first two lines on the next page. At the time we took this deposition did you not tell me that you just sat there and watched?

A: That is what I did. I told you just now.

Q: I think you have now stated, if I understood your testimony, or at least your testimony in response to Mr. Hart's questions, that you braced yourself.

A: I am sorry. I didn't know that is what you meant when you asked me this. It was unimportant. One of the reasons I hit my face was that I held onto the dashboard like this with my arms.

Q: Did you or did you not answer at that time that you just sat there and watched?

A: Yes.

Q: And then did you go on to say, "we knew there was a pretty good chance, and I just waited, because it wasn't really that long"?

A: Correct.

Q: It did happen fast then?

A: Yes. We were going awfully fast.

Q: You don't really know how fast?

A: All right. I won't say that.

Q: I have just a few more questions along the lines of your testimony in terms of just before the accident. You do not believe, if I understand your previous testimony, that Paula had any intention of running into the back of that snowplow?

MR. HART: I object to that as not material, the intention. I think maybe if the Court is considering overruling the objection that argument on this subject ought to be had out of the presence of the jury.

THE COURT: All right. Ladies and gentlemen, you may go to the jury room.

(The jury is now absent from the courtroom.)

MR. HART: If it please the Court, the basis for this objection is that the intention to have an accident or to cause injury is not a factor in willful and wanton disregard.

(Counsel continue their argument off the record.)

THE COURT: The objection will be sustained. It calls for speculation and conjecture on the part of the witness. You may bring back the jury.

(The jury is now present in the courtroom.)

Q: (by Mr. Wilton): Now, Miss Rasmussen, from your observation of Paula during the period of driving just before this, can you state to the jury whether or not she was paying attention to the road and the road conditions?

A: I can't say because I wasn't her. As far as I know, I guess.

Q: Do you know where she first saw the snowplow on the road?

A: About the same time I did. I told you we looked at each other and acknowledged it.

Q: And is it your testimony, then, that after seeing this that she then started to go to the left as though perhaps to pass the snowplow?

A: Not the exact moment. It was half a mile away or something. She kept going. This is speculation, but — could you ask me the question again?

Q: Do you recall her turning slightly to the left as though to go into the other lane, as though to pass the snowplow?

A: Just, if I did, it was very slightly. Not at the time we saw the snow-plow.

Q: It was after that?

A: I know that she checked it out, the possibility. She was looking. But she made no real swerve into the left lane.

Q: In terms of putting her brakes on do you know whether she ever put her brakes on?

A: No. I mean I didn't see her.

Q: You heard the officer's testimony that he found some skidmarks?

A: Yes.

Q: But you were simply unaware of whether the brakes were ever put on. Is that correct?

A: Yes.

Q: Now, this may sound like a foolish question to you, Miss Rasmussen, but I don't believe it to be. Do you believe you were going slower at the instant you hit the snowplow than the moment you were going down the incline?

A: Do you want my opinion?

Q: Yes.

A: Could you say the question again?

Q: Do you believe the car you were riding in as a passenger had slowed down any from the time it was coming around this bend here to the time it struck the snowplow?

A: It must have.

MR. WILTON: I have no further questions.

QUESTIONS

1. Do you think that Wilton's cross examination reduced the impact of Anne's testimony? What do you think was the impact of cross examination on the jury?

2. What was Wilton trying to accomplish by his detailed examination concerning the accident? Were the benefits to his position likely to be worth the costs?

3. On redirect, Hart went back to the deposition testimony used by Wilton to impeach Anne's testimony. Hart asked Anne to read the questions and answers that preceded her estimate of one city block. Turn back and reread that passage. How do you think that affected the jury?

4. As Anne testified, the jury was evaluating her not only as a witness, but as the potential recipient of their largess. It is for that reason that Wilton's handling of her was of tremendous practical importance. If he could show her to be a liar, then the jury might become quite unsympathetic, and consider the question of "payment" in cold and abstract terms. On the other hand, if he tried to show her to be a liar but instead showed her to be a young (now 19 years old) woman beleaguered by the defense attorney, the questions of "payment" and, indeed, of "willful and wanton" might be looked at in a different light by the jury. Do you think that Wilton successfully discredited Anne or her testimony, or did his questions create sympathy for Anne?

(d) Examination of plaintiff's physician

Hart had four more witnesses on damages (Anne's physician, the music director, and her parents) and two witnesses on "payment" (Paula and Dr. Graham). He decided to save Anne's mother for last, for tactical reasons that will be apparent when we see how she testified. Hart called the three other damages witnesses, and then Paula and Dr. Graham on "payment," and then Mrs. Rasmussen.

Hart called Anne's physician to testify after Anne's testimony was completed. Hart took him through the medical aspects of the case, stage by stage and detail by detail. He showed and explained some X-rays to the jury, taken shortly after the accident. He concluded his direct testimony with a discussion of Anne's current status and her prognosis.

In a brief cross examination, Wilton brought out that Anne's status might be improvable by surgery, but that Anne had not been to see him for over a year. The doctor resisted this line, indicating that there was some benefit in letting things settle for a year or more after traumatic injury to the face in order to see how well natural healing processes would do without surgery.

(e) Examination of the Colorado State University Band director

Anne had testified that the middle portion of her upper lip had been numb since about the time of the accident, and as a result, she had been unable to continue as a serious flutist. Her physician had testified that the numbness was an unavoidable consequence of certain suturing that had been required by the accident.

This set the stage for Anne's next witness, the director of the Colorado State University Band. He testified that Anne had participated in summer music programs at the University for about seven years. He had directed these programs and was quite impressed with her musical ability: "She was a very talented young lady, remarkable amount of ability on the instrument." Prior to the accident he had recommended her for a music scholarship, in the amount of two thousand dollars a year for four years. As a result of the inability to continue with the flute, this scholarship was not available to her.

(f) Examination of plaintiff's father

Hart's next witness was Anne's father. It so happened that he had a doctorate in educational psychology. In his testimony he described the continuing emotional and psychological effects the accident had had on his daughter. He discussed these changes in some detail. Though his manner was a bit detached, perhaps even clinical, the fact that it was his daughter he was discussing wasn't lost on the jury.

At this point, Hart also brought out the fact that Anne had been a candidate for high school homecoming queen in the two years preceding the accident. Hart introduced into evidence three photographs that Anne's father had taken during the two years preceding the accident along with three photographs that he had taken since that time.

(g) Examination of defendant Paula Graham

(1) Direct examination

Having pretty much completed his case on the damages issue (except for Mrs. Rasmussen's testimony), Hart now turned to "payment." He took the unusual step of calling the opposing party, Paula Graham, as his next witness. Her testimony on direct examination was as follows (you might notice that Hart's examination of Paula was mostly by leading questions; this was permitted because Paula was an adverse party, and would presumably say as little as possible in response to nonleading questions):

Q: Would you state your name, please?

A: Paula Graham.

Q: You are one of the defendants in this action?

A: Yes.

Q: The 1987 Tercel automobile you were driving on December 30, 1993, had been purchased for you by your father, had it not?

A: Yes.

Q: Did he also provide you with unlimited gasoline to put in the car, or were you on an allowance?

A: No, he didn't provide me. I had an allowance. But it was an allowance just like all kids have. It wasn't for gas. I could use it for gas. He didn't pay for the gas for the car.

Q: You paid for your own gasoline in the car?

A: Usually. He paid sometimes.

Q: But most of the time would it be fair to say that you paid for it yourself?

A: Uh huh, yes.

Q: And you heard Anne Rasmussen testify that when you left Fort Collins to go to Steamboat Springs late in December of 1994 that you had some Gasamat tokens that had been received as a Christmas gift. Do you recall her testifying to that?

A: Yes.

Q: Is that a correct statement that you had received a Christmas gift of some tokens to be used at the Gasamat?

A: I think so.

Q: And you considered that, how many of them were they? Do you recall?

A: I think there were three.

Q: And how does that work? Is it a kind of coin device that you use to get gas at a certain gas station?

A: Yes, Gasamat tokens. That is what you use instead of money. You pay money to get the tokens.

Q: And someone had made a gift to you, though, for Christmas of these tokens?

A: Yes, someone I drove around a lot.

Q: And did you consider this a nice and valuable gift?

A: What do you mean?

Q: Well, did you appreciate receiving it?

A: Oh, sure.

Q: It permitted you to, I assume, you are like my daughter, you like to drive your car as much as you can?

A: Yes.

Q: And a gift of tokens that you can purchase gas for permits you to drive that much further, doesn't it?

A: Yes. Well, you know, I had driven her around a lot. It was a nice thing to do, but it was about equal too.

Q: I see. You feel that while it was a nice gift because you had driven this girl around, perhaps it was somewhat in compensation?

A: Yes, that is how it was given, as a payment.

Q: As a payment?

A: No, not as payment for gas, not as a payment.

Q: Yes, I understand.

A: Okay.

Q: Now, I believe that you testified when I took your deposition that you and Anne talked about the expenses for gasoline to be incurred on this trip to Steamboat Springs and return. Is that correct?

A: I think I said I couldn't remember if we had a conversation or not.

Q: Well, do you recall indicating that you must have had the conversation because you had these Gasamat tokens and you were to buy the gas here and she was to buy it on the return trip?

A: Will you repeat that question please.

Q: Perhaps I can make it easier for you this way.

MR. HART: Your Honor, I think I will have that marked so we can refer to it as an exhibit.

(Plaintiffs' Exhibit U is marked for identification by the reporter.)

Q: Miss Graham, I hand you an exhibit that has now been marked Plaintiffs' Exhibit U and ask you if that is the deposition that was taken of you under oath on April 23, 1995, and signed by you before a notary public on May 10, 1995?

A: Yes.

Q: Now, would you please turn to page 12. Refer to a question on line 15 page 12. I was asking you questions at the time this deposition was taken, was I not?

A: Yes, you were.

Q: And will you please refer to line 15 and did I not ask you a question, "Do you recall Anne agreeing to pay for the gas coming back then, since you were paying for gas going over?" Now, would you read your answer to that question and see if that refreshes your recollection of your testimony at that time.

A: Out loud?

Q: No, just to yourself, please.

A: Yes, I have read it.

Q: Now, am I mistaken in reading that answer that you stated that "we must have said it" because you were buying the gas on the trip over and she was going to pay for it on the way back?

A: Well, we probably did say it. But I don't remember for sure, Mr. Hart.

Q: I understand. And, as a matter of fact, you had driven Anne as a passenger in your car on several trips prior to the trip to Steamboat Springs on December 28 of 1993, isn't that correct?

A: Yes.

Q: And each and every time that such a trip was made Anne paid for half of the gasoline on the trip?

A: Yes, except for one I can remember for sure. I charged it to my father. So neither one of us had to pay any.

Q: I see. But aside from that each and every trip you made together in your car, the 1987 Tercel automobile, she paid you a share of the gasoline expenses?

A: Yes.

Q: And as a matter of fact, on this trip on December 28 of 1993 you previously testified that you understood that she was going to pay for the gas on the trip back?

A: Yes, it was an agreement.

Q: I am sorry, I didn't hear.

A: Yes, it was an understood agreement.

MR. HART: I have no further questions, Your Honor, at this time.

(2) Cross examination

On cross examination, Wilton elicited the following testimony:

Q: On recalling any of these trips you took with the Plaintiff, in terms of gasoline, did you ever ask her to pay for half of the gasoline?

A: Do you mean while we were on the trip or at the gas station?

Q: At any time to the best of your knowledge do you recollect ever having asked her, that is, the plaintiff, Anne Rasmussen, to pay half of the gas?

A: Not to pay half. I might have sometime [at] a gas station when getting the gas asked her for some money if she was going to give it to me. And then when we came to get the gas I might say something like "Can I have the money?"

Q: In other words, you did have conversation in the past sometimes about this sort of thing?

A: Yes.

Q: Recalling your attention to the occasion of December 30, 1993, at the Gasamat, did you ever ask her for any payment of any kind at that time?

A: No.

Q: Recalling the entire trip from the Gasamat to, well, actually to the scene of the accident, did you ever ask her for payment on that trip?

A: No.

Q: In terms of gas, were you required to get gasoline at anytime during that trip between the time you left Fort Collins and the time the accident occurred?

A: I didn't get any gas. My father filled the tank in Steamboat.

Q: Was there any request for payment from Anne Rasmussen for payment for filling the tank in Steamboat?

A: No.

Q: These previous trips that Mr. Hart asked you about, would you describe the nature of these trips?

A: Social.

Q: And would you describe the trip to Steamboat Springs?

A: It was social.

MR. WILTON: No further questions.

(3) Redirect examination

Hart elicited the following testimony during redirect examination:

Q: As a matter of fact, Miss Graham, isn't it true that the understanding and agreement were that Anne, before you left Fort Collins on the trip to Steamboat Springs, was that Anne was to pay the gas on the trip back? She was to pay the gas for the trip back, isn't that true?

A: That was the understanding, is that what you said?

Q: Yes.

A: Yes.

Q: And as a matter of fact, you never started that trip back from Steamboat to Fort Collins, did you?

A: No, not in my car.

Q: So it is a fair statement that you never had occasion to ask her on that trip for her share of the expenses because that part of the trip was never taken?

A: Would you repeat the question, please?

Q: Since the understanding was that Anne was to buy the gas on the trip back from Steamboat to Fort Collins, and you never undertook that portion of the trip because of the collision, you didn't have occasion to ask her to buy the gas for the trip back?

A: No.

Q: Because there wasn't any trip back, isn't that the reason?

A: Yes, I guess so.

Q: Now, you were asked by your counsel the purpose for the trip from Steamboat to Craig and you used the word social. As a matter of fact, you wanted to get a key made to your parents' trailer, didn't you?

A: Yes.

Q: Now, as a matter of fact you had a key to your parents' trailer when you left Steamboat for Craig?

A: I had their key.

Q: So, what was the purpose of obtaining a key if you already had one?

A: I had their key. I was having one made for myself.

Q: And was this with your father's consent or knowledge?

A: No.

Q: Why did you want a key made for the trailer?

A: So when they left I would have a key.

Q: Had they already told you that they didn't want you staying in the trailer after they left?

A: See, the heater had broken and so there had been a lot of trouble with the fuses and stuff and they thought it might be dangerous to stay in there. So they didn't want us to stay there, no.

Q: So, as a matter of fact, the trip to Craig was not with your father's approval?

A: Well, I don't know if he approved of it, because I didn't ask him.

Q: You didn't want him to know about it, as a matter of fact, did you?

A: Not at the time, no.

Q: And as a matter of fact, you expected to get this key made for the purpose of utilizing the trailer after they had gone, although your father had indicated that he didn't want you to use it? Isn't that true?

A: That we wanted to use it after he was gone?

Q: Yes, without his knowledge?

A: Yes, we thought about it.

MR. HART: Thank you. I have nothing further, Your Honor.

MR. WILTON: No questions, Your Honor.

THE COURT: That is all. You may step down.

QUESTIONS

1. Did Hart's closing colloquy, concerning the intended deception of Paula's parents, disprove that Anne's presence on the trip to Craig was "social"? Did the purpose of the trip have a bearing on the question of "payment" within Colorado Guest Statute? If not, why did Hart go into it? Was that a wise tactical decision?

2. You should note that Hart did not pursue this question on his direct examination, and Wilton, of course, did not open the issue during his cross examination. Ordinarily, redirect examination is limited to topics addressed during cross examination, so a proper objection might have blocked Hart from pursuing this line of questioning. Why did Hart save this issue for redirect, instead of addressing it during direct examination? Do you think Hart intended all along to explore this issue and simply saved it for redirect? If so, was this a wise tactical decision?

(h) Examination of Roger Graham

Hart next called Dr. Graham. His major goal was to have Paula's father repeat his statement (set out above) that "at that age they are doing anything they can to raise a dollar for gasoline."

(i) Examination of plaintiff's mother

Hart's final witness was Elizabeth Rasmussen, Anne's mother. Her testimony was as follows:

Q: Would you state your name please?

A: My name is Elizabeth Rasmussen.

Q: Are you the mother of Anne Rasmussen?

A: Yes, I am.

Q: Mrs. Rasmussen, after the injury that was sustained by your daughter on December 30 of 1993, when did you first see her after that time?

A: When she arrived from Steamboat by ambulance. We got to the Presbyterian Hospital about four, and she arrived about five o'clock.

Q: Now, was that AM or PM?

A: PM.

Q: And that was on December 30, 1993?

A: Yes.

Q: And from that time until she had the surgery that has been testified to, how much of your time, if any, did you spend with her or in her presence?

A: I stayed at the medical center five days and five nights. I never left the hospital. I didn't even get out of my clothes.

Q: And during that five days and five nights did you have an opportunity to observe your daughter while she was in the hospital?

A: Yes, I certainly did.

Q: Can you describe to the jury her appearance when you first saw her after the injury?

A: Well, it is a horrible experience to see your beautiful daughter when you walk in there and there she is lying down and her first concern was for us. She asked —

Q: Just a moment. I think I have to confine your testimony to be responsive to my questions. I wanted you just to describe how she physically appeared to you?

A: Well, her face was very depressed, flat. Her upper teeth were hanging down in her mouth, all caked with blood. Her hair was streaked with blood. Her eyes had already become very black and red.

Q: Were you in her presence at any time prior to the surgery at which any procedures were undertaken in connection with the caring for her or treating her?

A: Do you mean me?

Q: Yes, were you present while nurses or doctors or interns were working with her?

A: Yes.

Q: Do you recall anything that stands out in your memory in connection with any of those procedures?

A: I think one of the most horrible things was listening to her cry out the night before her surgery. They had to scrub her mouth. It had all this decayed blood. It had all stayed on her teeth. And before they could take her into surgery the next morning it had to come off. They were scrubbing and I couldn't take it. I went out. And I could hear her crying and screaming down the hall as they cleaned those teeth.

Q: Now, did you observe anything about your daughter, Anne, relative to her face or head during the five days and five nights you were in the hospital, concerning her keeping it covered or uncovered?

A: Yes, she kept a cloth on her face almost all the time until the surgery on Friday. She just asked us to wet the cloth all the time and we wrang it out and she laid it on her face and she laid there with her face never uncovered until the surgery.

Q: To your knowledge when was the first time your daughter, Anne, saw herself after the injury?

A: It was probably two or three days after the surgery and Dr. Mammel had suggested that we get her up on her feet a little more. And she was using an electric walker at the time. And so I took her to the sink in the bathroom to scrub her teeth and she looked up in the mirror. This was the first time she ever looked at her face.

Q: What occurred at that time?

A: Well, she immediately broke down and went to pieces. And I got her back to bed as best I could by myself there. We covered the mirror. After that she never went to the bathroom without a magazine on the mirror and we kept it covered and she never looked again.

Q: Can you describe your daughter's progress after the second time that she was in the hospital and then came home, and then from that time on up to today? Can you describe the progress that she had made in connection with her appearance and her injury?

A: Well, the first thing I think she lost her youth. She was a teenager and suddenly she was an adult. I think this is the greatest loss to me that the accident did to her. She was a bubbling, laughing seventeen-year-old teenager. And in the hospital she had to witness death. A man died right beside her.

Q: I don't think that, I am sorry, but I understand you would think that is material.

A: But to me overnight she had to grow up. She had to witness things and she lost that youth just over night. She was no longer a teenager. She didn't smile. She wasn't as happy. She was withdrawn and stayed in her room, like her father said, a lot more. She had headaches, stomachaches.

Q: You heard your husband, and Anne's father, testify concerning what he had observed. Would you confirm everything that he testified in his observations?

A: Very definitely.

MR. HART: You may inquire.

Wilton asked only a few, brief questions.
The witness was excused, and Hart said: "The plaintiff rests, Your Honor."
Hart had completed his case.

ii. Defense motions for directed verdict

You have read most of the testimony on the two liability issues, "payment," and "willful and wanton." As previously discussed on each issue Hart had to produce enough evidence to *permit* a reasonable juror to find in his favor, or lose that issue. After Hart rested, Wilton moved that a directed verdict for defendant be granted on plaintiff's first and third claims for relief. This motion raised the same issues as the summary judgment motion which Judge Shannon had granted and then changed his mind about immediately before trial. The significant difference was that the summary judgment addressed the question of whether plaintiff would be able to produce enough evidence at trial on the issue of payment to permit that issue to go to the jury. At the time of the directed verdict motion, there was no longer any reason to guess at the evidence Hart would present on the issue; at the time of the motion, Hart had completed his presentation and the question before the court was whether the evidence Hart had in fact presented on "payment" was sufficient to get that issue to the jury.

Wilton's argument at this point was that Hart had been given his opportunity to produce all the evidence he had on "payment." Wilton argued that Hart had not introduced *any* evidence that the trip was not merely social. Therefore, the jury would have to find that the trip was social, and if they found that, they could not find that payment had been made. Hart responded that there was substantial evidence supporting an inference of a serious, explicit agreement that Anne make a certain payment to Paula and therefore a reasonable juror could find a payment sufficient to satisfy the statute.

The court denied the motion to direct a verdict on the first claim for relief.

Wilton also sought a directed verdict on the "willful and wanton" issue. Wilton argued that "willful and wanton" (applicable if there had been no payment) required proof that Paula purposely committed an act knowing that it created an undue risk of an accident. Can you guess at Hart's response?

The Court also denied Wilton's motions to direct a verdict on plaintiff's "willful and wanton" claim (plaintiff's third claim for relief).

By this time, two full days of trial had occurred. The Court recessed for the evening.

iii. Defendant's case

Most of the issues Wilton wished to cover had in fact been covered during the presentation of plaintiff's case. Wilton planned on using his witnesses for the purpose simply of driving a few points home.

(a) Examination of the driver of the snowplow

First he called the driver of the snowplow. Wilton used him to show the condition of the road at the time of the accident, the fact that the snowplow had no flashing lights, and the fact that at the point of impact the snowplow was not even dented, and indeed was hardly even scratched.

On cross examination, Hart brought out the fact that the impact actually moved the snowplow, despite the fact that it weighed over twenty-four thousand pounds. Hart also elicited testimony that the impact was so forceful that the driver was knocked against the back of the cab, broke a rib (confirmed by X-rays), and, even at the time of trial, had to wear a back brace to do manual labor. Hart also elicited testimony that in the eleven years he had been operating the snowplow, the Tercel was the only car that had run into him.

On redirect, Wilton brought out the fact that during those eleven years, a number of cars had just barely avoided hitting him.

(b) Examination of the mechanic

Wilton's second witness was the foreman of a Fort Collins Toyota body repair shop. Wilton had hoped that he would testify, based on pictures of the Tercel after the accident, that it had not been moving quickly at the time of the accident. The witness had not actually seen or worked on Paula's car. Hart objected that the witness was not sufficiently expert to give such testimony based solely on photographs of the automobile; Hart's objection was sustained. Wilton was able to have him describe the part of the dash that Anne's face had struck.

On cross examination of Wilton's expert, Hart was allowed to elicit testimony that the speedometer was the largest instrument on the dash and that it had a fairly central location. This supported Anne's testimony that she knew how fast Paula had been driving because she had been able to observe the speedometer.

(c) Examination of defendant Paula Graham

Wilton's next witness was Paula. She testified on two matters: "payment" and the accident. As to "payment," Wilton pursued Paula's friendship with Anne. He also had Paula go over the informality of the arrangements for reimbursement. Wilton's major concentration, however, was on the facts surrounding the accident. Once again, testimony was elicited regarding the speed of the car and the respective locations of the car and the snowplow when Paula first saw the snowplow.

On cross examination, Hart briefly examined Paula regarding "payment," covering some of the ground previously covered. He also went over the facts of the accident, concentrating on some inconsistencies between her testimony on direct examination and the statements she had made at her deposition concerning the crucial facts of her speed and distance from the snowplow at the time she first sighted it.

(d) Examination of defendant Paula Graham's mother

Finally, Wilton called Paula's mother, who testified that Anne had been invited up as a guest, and that she was not expected to contribute to the cost of the food used at the trailer. On cross examination, Hart tried to get Mrs. Graham to concede that, particularly in view of Paula's recent mononucleosis, she and Dr. Graham would have been somewhat reluctant to let Paula stay at the trailer after they returned to Fort Collins if she had not brought a friend to stay with her. By this reasoning, Anne's agreement to stay at the trailer with Paula would then have amounted to a benefit to the Grahams, or at least to Paula, in the nature of a "payment." Mrs. Graham, however, steadfastly refused to make this concession.

Wilton had no other witnesses, and rested his case. Hart had no rebuttal case. Accordingly the evidence was closed.

4. GIVING THE CASE TO THE JURY

a. Instructions to the Jury

Before the jury retires to consider its verdict, it must be given instructions by the judge indicating just what questions it must decide. In order to resolve a disputed issue it often is necessary for the jury not only to reconstruct past events from the evidence placed before it, but also to determine whether those events fit a particular legal standard or definition. For instance, in *Rasmussen v. Graham* one of the important issues was "payment." What constitutes "payment" within the meaning of the guest statute is a question of law, but whether "payment" was made in a given case is a question of fact to be decided by the jury. Before the jury can decide that question, however, it must be instructed as to the legal meaning of payment. That instruction must come from the judge.

The jury can be told exactly what factors to consider in deciding whether there was payment, or it can be left largely, or somewhat, or a little bit, on its own. The more precisely the judge defines the meaning of the term "payment," the more the jury's function is reduced to that of merely the reconstructor of past events. The more loosely the question is defined, the more the jury is allowed to add value judgments to its decision, and the broader the inferential process the jury will engage in. For example, the judge could define the question quite narrowly in either of the following ways:

> 1. "Payment" refers to any item of pecuniary benefit. I instruct you that if you find that the plaintiff either gave or promised to give any item of pecuniary benefit to the defendant, and further find that the giving of that item was related to defendant's providing transportation for the plaintiff, or was made to help defray any costs arising out of that transportation, then you must find that payment has been made.

> *[alternative instruction]*

> 2. "Payment" refers to the exchange of benefits. In order to find that payment has been made, you must find, first, that the plaintiff gave or

promised to give defendant an item of pecuniary benefit, and second, that the purpose of giving this benefit was to induce the defendant to make a trip she would not otherwise have made, and third, that the defendant's purpose in making the trip was the procurement of the benefit.

You will note that these instructions will likely yield different results on the facts of this case. In each, the judge has given the jurors a series of three narrow, "factual" type questions. Each of these two instructions gives a fairly precise (though different) definition of the statutory word "payment," and by doing so allocates to the judge (and away from the jury) a good bit of the decision-making process.

As an example of a very general instruction, broader than is likely to be given, consider the following:

3. If you find that the plaintiff has given or promised to give to the defendant an item of benefit such that a reasonable person would not consider the commencement of this lawsuit an ungrateful act, then you must find that payment has been made.

The first two instructions each represented a decision by the judges of what sort of activities were sufficient to satisfy the legislative control of ingratitude (assuming, of course, that the purpose of the statute was the protection of generous hosts against ungrateful guests). In the third instruction, the decision of how much payment should be required before the suit can be allowed is left to the jury. The values that will be consulted to answer this question will be the jurors'.

Throughout the entire case, Wilton had worked at getting the judge to decide the question of payment, while Hart worked at getting it to the jury. At the close of evidence, Wilton once again moved for a directed verdict on plaintiff's first claim for relief. His motion was denied. Wilton, Hart, and the judge then discussed what instructions should be given to the jury. At the beginning of the trial Hart and Wilton each had submitted proposed instructions. At the conclusion of the evidence, each attorney was given an opportunity to argue why each of his proposed instructions should be used, and also why his opponent's proposed instructions were improper.

The judge's job of choosing the best instructions, formerly fraught with great danger of reversible error, has been made much simpler by the development of pattern jury instructions, now available in a number of states. In these states the state Supreme Court has been authorized to appoint a committee, which in turn drafts model instructions for common fact issues. Colorado has such a system, and Colorado Rule of Civil Procedure 51.1 provides:

(1) In instructing a jury in a civil case, the court shall use such instructions as are contained in Colorado Jury Instructions (C.J.I.) as are applicable to the evidence and the prevailing law....

After Hart and Wilton had finished their arguments on the instructions, the judge ruled on which instructions he would give to the jury. Based on the Colorado pattern instructions, the judge approved an instruction on the issue of payment worded as follows:

No person transported by the operator of a motor vehicle as his guest, without payment for such transportation shall be entitled to recover damages from such operator for injury in case of accident, unless such accident shall have been proximately caused by negligence of such operator consisting of a willful and wanton disregard of the rights of others.

A person is a guest when she is being transported in a vehicle at the invitation, express or implied, of the operator of the vehicle without payment for such transportation. *The payment may be cash or any benefit which is sufficiently real, tangible or substantial so as to have been an inducing cause for the transportation.* [Emphasis added.]

Hart and Wilton then each made a formal statement for the record, setting forth the basis for his objections to the court's instructions.

The court was then called to order, the jury returned to the courtroom, and the judge read the approved instructions to the jury.

QUESTIONS

1. Compare the approved instruction on payment with alternative instructions one, two, and three. Is the approved instruction narrow or broad? Does it leave enough to the jury? Too much?

2. What specific factual questions does the instruction put to the jury? Do you think that this instruction accurately defines "payment," as that term is used in the guest statute?

3. You have now been presented with most of the evidence that was given the actual jury. Based on that evidence, and equipped with the foregoing instruction, how would you (as a juror) go about answering the payment question? Do you have enough information to answer it rationally?

b. Closing Arguments

After the instructions were read to the jury, Wilton and Hart were permitted to make their closing arguments.[14] Many litigators believe the closing argument is the most important period of the trial. Examination of witnesses is conducted with an eye towards eliciting (or extracting) the testimony the lawyer needs for her closing argument. Indeed, for many, the entire preparation of the case is aimed towards providing the attorney with the most effective closing argument.

By prior arrangement, each of the attorneys was given one hour for his closing argument.

i. Plaintiff's closing arguments

After a general introduction, Hart divided his time among negligence, payment, and damages, in that order. Following are some excerpts from his argument, showing his introduction, his discussions of payment, and his final remarks made in relation to damages.

> MR. HART: If it please the Court, ladies and gentlemen of the jury:
>
> I feel that arguments by counsel after you have heard all of the testimony and the evidence in the case certainly is at the very best anticlimax and may not serve too much of a purpose. I think you understand that what I say to you in my closing argument is not evidence. I hope you understand by this time I am an advocate. I am here on behalf of the plaintiff. Mr. Wilton also is an advocate for the defendants and will present their position to you.
>
> You six people on the jury, aside from the Court and perhaps the Court personnel, are really the only impartial people in this courtroom in connection with this matter. You are the ones, therefore, who should make the decision and who should make the determination from the testimony and evidence that has been presented in the case.
>
> If, however, I can make what seems to be a complex case really as simple as it is, then I could serve some purpose in making a closing argument to you. This is the reverse, I suppose, of what people think lawyers do. Usually we try to make the simple complex.
>
> There is an old New England saying that three Philadelphia lawyers are a match for the devil. But I would like to try to make in this case what appears to be a complex case as simple as I think it is.[15]

---

[14] In most jurisdictions (but not Colorado), the closing arguments are made before rather than after the instructions are read. What are the advantages and disadvantages of permitting the attorneys to argue after, rather than before, the judge instructs the jury?

[15] What has Hart hoped to accomplish with his arguments to this point?

I would like to first suggest some general considerations to you in considering this case. When you check in as jurors in a case you do not check out your common sense. The fact that the court has instructed you that you may consider only the testimony and evidence in this case, but you may consider any reasonable inference or inferences that can be drawn from such testimony and evidence so long as it is based upon reason and common sense. And this really is the strength of our jury system, because there isn't any body of people who bring to this court, no judge, no lawyer, no arbitrator, the reservoir of human experience and common sense that you six people do. So remember you are not confined precisely to the testimony and the evidence in this case. You may make reasonable inferences from that testimony and evidence based upon common sense and reason.

. . . .

The principal affirmative defense in this case I am sure will be the claim that Anne Rasmussen at the time of this collision was a legal guest in the automobile, in the Graham automobile.

Now, notice I used the term legal guest, and I will use that throughout because that is the test. It is not social guest but what laymen consider to be the usual and customary practice among friends. It is what the Court defines for you as a guest in this case. So I am going to refer to the situation was she a legal guest.

Now, have the defendants, by a preponderance of the evidence, established that Anne Rasmussen was a legal guest in the Graham automobile at the time involved in this case? The Court has instructed you that if a person, in effect, pays for transportation as an inducement, now not the inducement, but an inducement, there can be more than one inducement for transportation. The Court has instructed you that if a person makes a payment which is either cash or any benefit that is sufficiently real, tangible or substantial as to constitute an inducement for the transportation, that person isn't a legal guest.[16]

There can be many inducements for transportation. I will not deny that one of the inducements for this transportation was the fact that the girls were friends and they were going off for a weekend to enjoy themselves and enjoy their company. But that in itself is not sufficient to take her out of that category and put her in this category because there were other inducements for that transportation. And from the testimony and evidence I think you can reasonably infer this with clarity and force. And I would like to give you some examples.

---

[16] Is Hart's argument consistent with your reading of the Colorado Supreme Court cases discussed in the summary judgment section of this book?

They had a course of conduct between these two girls. It had occurred before. It was an understood agreement, that was Miss Graham's testimony, that Anne was to pay a part of the cost of the transportation. Not gratuitously, not hospitably as a guest would do. There was an understood agreement between them. It was to such an extent they discussed it before they left on the trip to Steamboat. And it was agreed at that time that consistent with their course of conduct Anne would make payment for gasoline on the return trip.

It was clear that through that course of conduct and through the conversations and agreements these girls had reached, that Anne expected to pay and that Paula expected to receive payment. Do you recall her testifying that if it was Anne's time to pay she would ask Anne for the money to pay in the filling station. This was not gratuitous, single payment, where on this particular trip Anne said, "Well, let me help you with the gas," and Paula, "Well, I don't think you should. Well, all right, if you want to." This is not that type of situation at all.

The situation about the Gasamat tokens, and again I didn't put these words in Miss Graham's mouth. She volunteered these things, which I think gives it more force. I didn't try to drag these things out of her. She said about the Gasamat tokens that she received at Christmastime, well, that it wasn't really too much of a gift because as it came out the Osterle girl that gave the tokens to her had been driven around quite a bit by Paula and I think she said she just felt that this was payment for the gasoline that she had used in driving this girl.

The tank of her car was almost always empty her father testified and she liked to drive the car. Do you think she was induced to go places with Anne other than being paid for driving, not paid for driving but paid for gasoline which enabled her to use the car more than she would otherwise? Is that a tangible and real benefit to this teenage girl of 17 with the empty gas tank? Isn't it sufficient to be an inducing cause of the transportation?

Who knows Paula Graham better than anyone else in respect to monetary matters and gasoline and automobiles, than her father? We know that from human experience, that her father does. And what was her father's testimony in this connection? And I don't want to be mistaken so I would like to read it to you. This is a portion of the deposition taken under oath which was read into evidence and he answered the question.

I said, "And on the contrary if your daughter went with Anne it works in reverse that your daughter contributed half of the expenses of the transportation." And he said, "Yes. I really think that at that age they are doing anything they can to raise a dollar for gasoline."

Now do you think it is unreasonable of me to suggest that you can draw reasonable inferences from these facts in this case that the promise and expectation of payment on that return trip was a benefit sufficiently real and tangible to be an inducement for that transportation?

[Hart ultimately turned to damage issues.]

Never before this day have I been able to state to a jury conscientiously and without fear of exaggerating that you could put any amount of money in this blank and you would not compensate Anne Rasmussen for her physical and emotional pain and suffering that she has suffered and will suffer for the rest of her life as the result of this injury. You could put in $500,000 and it wouldn't compensate her. And I am not talking about punishing Paula Graham. You shouldn't consider that, whether her conduct is willful or wanton or not. It should be a compensation to this girl. Six years of her life have been devoted to becoming accomplished on the flute and interest in that is gone. A happy-go-lucky, friendly, sociable girl, now withdrawn. You can't cover up all the mirrors in life. You are going to have to look. And this isn't something God or nature did to her. Someone did it to her by a heedless act. Every time she puts on her makeup in the morning, combs her hair, takes her makeup off at night, takes out a mirror to put on lipstick, catches a glimpse of her profile in the shop windows, buys a dress and looks in one of those three-way mirrors that lets her see her profile, or watches a television set and compares a person's profile with hers. Words of mine can't express the shocking thing that happened to her at the worst possible time. Look at her pictures before that injury. Just look at those pictures and understand and she was 17 years of age at the time it occurred. At 17 a hickey on her face can send a teenager into a week's retirement. Think of the shock, the emotional shock to her that is going to be with her the rest of her natural life. There isn't any amount of money that can compensate her for that. It is a lot worse than the physical pain. You can take pills and aspirin and do things like that to alleviate physical pain. You can't alleviate emotional and traumatic shock she took. It is ten times worse than the physical pain. And I must caution you, do not exceed, if you unanimously agree you could put in $500,000, don't do it. We have only asked for $190,000 in the complaint for her, and that is all you should put in your verdict.

Thank you.

ii. Defendant's closing arguments

Next came Wilton's closing argument:

MR. WILTON: Ladies and gentlemen of the jury.

I want to reiterate a couple of things about my closing statement to you so that you will understand why I am even standing here before you.

First of all, it is very clear that what I say to you now is not evidence in the case and Mr. Hart indicated that and you must also understand one other thing that perhaps was not so clearly brought out by Mr. Hart, on behalf of the plaintiffs. And that is that it is impossible for an attorney to work on a person's case for a period of time necessary to prepare and to present it to the Court and to the jury in a logical, meaningful way without developing a tremendous amount of feeling for your clients and their position on the case. I think it is obvious from your hearing Mr. Hart's last few remarks that he has developed this very strong sense of loyalty and responsibility to his client. And I think that can only be admirable in that regard.

Ladies and gentlemen of the jury, my problem is that there are two sides to every lawsuit. I, too, and I hope the evidence will show that, have worked very hard and diligently to try to present evidence and facts to the Court and have worked with my clients who are seated here, the other parties in the case. The parties we haven't talked about in the closing argument yet. And unfortunately for me, I guess I have developed a great deal of sense of responsibility and loyalty to my clients and I feel that they are entitled to my best efforts. And in talking to you about the final things I think are critical matters in this particular case from their standpoint.[17]

Because you see there can be no justice done in this case unless it is justice to both parties. I don't know whether you recall from your looking at the scales of justice with the lady blindfolded, but when she holds them out there are two sides. And they are to be balanced if justice is to be done. So we must determine what is justice, not only to the plaintiff in this action but what is justice to the defendant in this case.

Now, one of the things that we have got to start with, and I want to call back to your attention the time when we were selecting the jury. One of the most difficult things for me to do is to stand in front of you ladies and gentlemen when there are photographs that have been admitted, such as the ones Mr. Hart has offered in evidence, some of which were taken at his request, that were brought before you here for comparative purposes. I hope you will recall that in my opening argument I indicated to you that there was no doubt in our mind, and when I speak of our, I am speaking of the defendants, there was no doubt in our mind that this girl was injured and hurt badly. I indicated to you that this wasn't our position in this case. Mr. Hart is absolutely right, Dr. Mammel was brought onto the witness stand and he testified and we had the right to have other doctors come and testify if we thought this was the reason we were going to be here to bring this case in front of you. But this wasn't the reason, not to convince you that those photographs aren't absolutely accurate. And when we speak of common sense, ladies and gentlemen of the jury, you have had the opportunity to observe Miss Rasmussen here in the courtroom yourselves. And I credit you

---

[17] Doesn't the preceding paragraph sound almost apologetic? Does its tone help defendant's case?

with the common sense to be able to determine for yourselves the impact that this accident has had upon this girl's life. But we wouldn't be here if it weren't for what we consider to be the liability aspect of this case.

And once again, I asked two questions when we were selecting a jury and it was very important to me to know what your answers were at that time. And I think you will now see why. One of the questions was if the judge instructs you that sympathy and prejudice for or against any party has no part in this case, and that ladies and gentlemen is in instruction No. 9. And perhaps I had better read it again because it is so important. I am placed in the position of asking you to find the verdict for the defendant, Paula Graham. I am placed in that position when obviously there has been a severe and debilitating injury to plaintiff in this case. And every natural tendency that we have would cry out, or something that we would call, I think, sympathy for her. As her mother put it herself, and put it quite well, when she testified this girl has lost her youth. It is a very, very difficult thing to measure in terms of dollars and cents under any circumstance. But this was the primary thing. And if I came up before you and said no she didn't have these injuries, no she wasn't hurt, first of all I have got to be a liar at best and, secondly, I have got to be misleading you in the worst sort of way. We are not arguing that part of the case. But I know that from the questions and the way that you answered them when we were selecting the jury that you pledged to follow the Court's instructions and this is going to be the most difficult part of the case for a person sitting there in the jury. Because there are going to be some instructions, and I will review two or three of them with you, that are going to be difficult for you to follow. But you pledged when you took your oath as jurors that you would follow the instructions of the Court and I have to, and always had to, rely on that fact.

So the first one as I indicated is No. 9. You must not be governed or influenced by sympathy or prejudice for or against any party in this case.

And I must at this time ask you to review that pledge on behalf of my clients, the defendants here, because I don't think there can be any prejudice against the plaintiff in this case. I must ask you to review this pledge that you will not allow sympathy to be the governing thing in this case and that you will follow the instructions of law.

Now, as Mr. Hart mentioned, Colorado has got a guest statute. The Court has instructed you as to what this guest statute said. And I will want to review it. That is why we are here, in our opinion, ladies and gentlemen. That is what this case has all been about in the first place, the key and the crux. And I am not suggesting that all of these instructions aren't to be read and all to be considered as a whole. But I am suggesting to you, ladies and gentlemen, that there are a couple of real key points here that have to be decided by you. We can talk about a lot of other things, but when it gets right down to it these are going to be the things that are going to basically influence your decision in whether you find for the plaintiffs, and award money damage to them, or find for the defendant. Because we believe you will be following the instructions of the Colorado law.

Now, let's say you don't like what the guest statute said. Let's say you don't think that is right when somebody is a passenger in somebody else's vehicle and they are a guest in that vehicle that the only way they can recover is if that driver was willful and wanton and disregarded the rights and the safety of that person. Maybe you disagree with that. Maybe you don't think that should be the law. I can tell you candidly, ladies and gentlemen, that there are some instructions in here that I do not agree with. But these are the instructions that are to guide you in your deliberation.

[Wilton then briefly discussed the question of simple negligence. While he argued that Paula had not been negligent at all, he conceded that reasonable people might well come to a contrary conclusion. He then discussed the payment issue.]

What do you have to find then, if you agree with me that it was just passive inattention or ordinary or simple negligence, that was all that really occurred here, if you would agree with me on that data, then what do you have to find? You have to determine whether or not she was a guest as used in these instructions.

We turn now to Instruction No. 23 when we get to the question of the guest. I am certain you will have to refer to this when you deliberate on this case. This is the definition of guest. A "person is a guest when she is being transported in a vehicle at the invitation, expressed or implied, of the operator of the vehicle without payment for such transportation. The payment may be cash or any benefit which is sufficiently real, tangible or substantial so as to have been an inducing cause for the transportation."

Now, the way I interpret the word *induce* is that it must have been something to do with the reason that this girl was transported from Fort Collins to Steamboat Springs, Colorado.

Okay. Let's examine the exact facts of the case. Was she in the car as a passenger? Yes, she was seated in the righthand side. We can all agree to that. How did she get into the car in the first place? She was invited by Paula Graham to spend a weekend skiing with her at Steamboat Springs, with her and her family. She packed up her goods and came over and spent the night with Paula the night before they went to Steamboat Springs. But even before that she packed her skis on the Graham car that was preceding and had already gone over to Steamboat Springs. This is how we are getting from Fort Collins to Steamboat Springs. Do we have any payment at this point? Of course not. There is no cash payment involved in this case at all as a matter of fact. So what we have to deal with is was this offer to do something, did it have anything to do with the fact that she went from Steamboat Springs, Colorado, to Craig and back? Or even if you want to carry it further, to Steamboat Springs, to Craig, back to Steamboat Springs and then, no, she never got back.

So what we have to do is figure how did it arise. There was an invitation a week or so before. Staying overnight as a guest at the Graham home. Packing the car. The skis already having gone and they drive the car. What is the first thing they do? They start out on their trip from Dartmouth Trail in the south part of Fort Collins at the Graham home. They drive north to Larimer and they have started their trip. And on their way they stopped to get some gas. Who put the gas in the car? Once again dealing with good friends here. Somebody that has the tokens. They put the things in the car. Whose is that? That is the defendant's car. And then there is a claimed conversation that there was an agreement on Anne's part that she offered to pay for half of the gas and that half of the gas she paid for was on the return trip.

I think this is real important, that the only offer that Anne made that was discussed or understood in this case, the only offer she made was to pay the gas for the return trip.

Okay. What did the girls do? They went to Steamboat Springs and got there, and once again Paula and Anne were staying as guests of the parents. Once again we're not talking about guests in the car here, but guests in the general social sense. They were guests. They went to the ski slope and messed around as young kids do.

You remember the previous testimony that there was never any expectation for payment if the girls were riding around Fort Collins or when they were so-called driving around town. There was never any expectation of payment of those trips. There was never any agreement to pay for any of those kind of trips at those times. I can't remember any testimony on that. There was no expectation of payment in Steamboat Springs for driving around that occurred there. This was not a part of the trip over or back. And in fact, what did happen, the next day when the car wouldn't start, who put gas in the car? It was Dr. Graham. He put gas in the car, the gas that was put in the car and what gas was used when they went over to Craig, Colorado. The gas presumably, and again I hate to get to this kind of understanding, because who knows which came from the Gasamat or was put in at the station or what not. But there was no conversation about paying for any gas while messing around and using the car, that had been used for other means, in their drive to Craig, Colorado.

In other words, did this payment have any inducing cause whatsoever to make this trip from Steamboat to Craig and back? These were two good friends. Would the trip not have been made if, for instance, Anne had said,

"I am not going to pay you to go over there. I am not going to pay my half. This isn't the trip that I agreed to pay for. I agreed to pay for half of the gas on the trip to Fort Collins to Steamboat and back," or maybe just on the trip back. Was there any agreement of any kind that induced this and, in fact, ladies and gentlemen of the jury, can one imagine, can [one] ask this question, how can you answer this question if this was an inducing cause? Can we say that Anne would have been asked to leave the vehicle if in fact she had said at the Gasamat station, "Gee, I am broke. I can't pay you." Or, "Gee, I don't want to pay you because I have other commitments for my money."

Her skis were over there. They were already on the trip. The car was packed. Did this have anything to do with the fact that those two girls were going to Steamboat Springs, Colorado? And if you take it one step further, and the trip that the accident happened on, did it have anything whatsoever to do with the trip from Steamboat to Craig and back?

I ask you, ladies and gentlemen of the jury, I have analyzed this case and looked at these same facts that you have heard over and over and over again, and I have read this law. This law was known to us beforehand and it talks about payment may be cash. There is no cash payment or any benefit which is sufficiently tangible or substantial payment so as to have been the inducing cause to take this girl over there. It had to be a benefit to Anne if a benefit to anybody. Anne didn't even have to put the gas in to make the trip from Steamboat to Craig. Paula's dad put it in.

I have looked at these things and I believe in terms of our common-sense analysis of two high school friends who were friends first, and I seriously doubt if their friendship started on the basis of: "I will be your friend if you pay half of my gas." You are first friends and then you offer to do things that friends will do.

Again Mr. Hart and I ask you to consider a common-sense aspect of this thing and determine whether or not this young lady at the time and place of this was not a guest as defined by Instruction No. 23.

QUESTIONS

1. Hart and Wilton strongly, indeed passionately, differed on the payment issue. Did they hold different views of what events had actually occurred? Or was their difference caused by differing views on the applicable law? If the latter, should the correct view of the applicable law be left to the choice of the jury or is that more appropriately a judge's function? Did the instructions resolve this difference?

2. Did the closing arguments help the jury with the question of "payment"? If the jury is really being asked to resolve a question of statutory interpretation, shouldn't the attorneys have made arguments concerning the proper interpretation of the statute as well as the facts supporting their view?

3. If you were a juror, how would you have defined "payment"? Based on the instruction, and forgetting the excerpts from the appellate cases, how would you have voted on the "payment" issue?

c. The Jury's Verdict

After closing arguments, the bailiff was instructed to escort the jurors to the jury room, and to leave them there for their deliberation. They were allowed to take the following items into the jury room with them:

1. Typewritten copies of the instructions, prepared for them by the court;
2. Notes they might have taken during the presentation of the evidence;[18]
3. Documents and other real evidence that had been introduced into evidence; and
4. Verdict forms, on which the jury could record its verdict.

Most often the jury is asked to return a "general verdict." This consists of a simple statement by the jury, either that the jury finds for the plaintiff, for a certain sum, or that the jury finds for the defendant. No explanation and no further elaboration is required of the jury. Where only a general verdict is required the jury will ordinarily be given two pieces of paper by the judge. Each will have the usual caption. One will state "We, the jury, find for plaintiff and against defendant in the amount of $___.__," and the other, "We, the jury, find for defendant." Each will have a space for the date and the signature of the foreman of the jury.

Most jurisdictions permit the use of the Special Verdict. *See, e.g.,* Fed. R. Civ. P. 49(a). With this device, the jury is asked a series of specific questions. After the jury returns its answers to these questions, the judge will frame the judgment in accordance with the jury's answers. It is generally assumed that the jury will be less likely to give vent to its sympathies if it is asked narrow and specific questions rather than the general question asked by the general verdict. The conventional wisdom is that a jury is less likely to return a sympathy verdict for plaintiff if it is asked specific questions, rather than simply being asked which party should prevail, and if plaintiff prevails, how money should she be awarded.

A third type of verdict is really a compromise between the first two. This is the General Verdict accompanied by Interrogatories. *See* Fed. R. Civ. P. 49(b). Here the jury is asked in general terms who should win. In addition, however, the jury is also asked some specific questions. An inconsistency between the jury's

---

[18] In many jurisdictions, jurors are not permitted to take notes. In others, the question is left to the trial judge's discretion.

answers to the specific questions and its general verdict will suggest that it failed to follow the judge's instructions. In such a situation the judge may return the case to the jury, set the case for an entire retrial, or ignore the jury's general verdict and enter judgment on the basis of the answers to the interrogatories.

In our case, the jury was asked to return a general verdict but also was asked to answer a special interrogatory: Was the plaintiff transported as defendant's guest, "without payment therefor"? After closing arguments, the jurors were given the appropriate documents and then escorted to the jury room by the bailiff. Their first order of business was the selection of a foreman. The foreman's only formal authority is to be spokesman for the jury, and as such to sign the verdict form. The foreman usually will turn out also to be the informal leader of the group.

After the foreman was selected by the jurors, their deliberations began. We know very little about what was actually said in the jury room, but we can guess at what took place. The first step in reaching a verdict was probably a discussion and an informal vote on liability. Inasmuch as Colorado, like most other states, requires that a jury verdict must be unanimous, it would not make any sense to go to the question of the amount of damages until there was unanimous agreement on whether the defendant should pay any damages. If there were any disagreement on liability, the next step would be for the jurors to read very carefully through the pertinent instructions and then to discuss with one another why the evidence did or did not support liability. If the jurors agree that there should be liability, the process must then be gone through again on the issue of damages.

After about three hours in the jury room, the foreman called for the bailiff, and informed him that the jury had reached a verdict. The bailiff informed the judge, and the attorneys and parties were quickly assembled in the courtroom. The jury then filed into the courtroom, and the following exchange occurred:

> THE COURT: Has the jury reached a verdict?
> FOREMAN: Yes, your honor.
> THE COURT: And was that verdict unanimous?
> FOREMAN: Yes, your honor.
> THE COURT: Will you please hand your verdict to the bailiff?

The signed verdict form was handed to the bailiff, who read it as follows: "We, the jury, find for the plaintiff and against the defendant in the amount of $97,000." The special interrogatory was answered by a finding that Anne was not Paula's guest.[19]

---

[19] The jury had also had been asked whether Paula had been negligent and whether she had acted with "willful and wanton" disregard of Anne's rights. Both these questions were also answered "yes" by the jury. But after the jury had been discharged, it was discovered that the jury had

Wilton, who was a bit surprised by the verdict, asked that the jury be polled. The judge then asked each juror if that were the verdict he had approved. Each of the six replied affirmatively. Wilton had lost.

5. POST-VERDICT PROCEDURE

a. Entry of Judgment

The verdict itself has no coercive power. It is simply a statement of what the jury thought the appropriate result should be. Fed. R. Civ. P. 58 provides, however, that "Upon a general verdict of a jury, ... the clerk, unless the court otherwise orders, shall forthwith prepare, sign and enter the judgment without awaiting any direction by the court."

The bailiff carried the signed verdict form to the clerk's office. There the clerk of the court completed the following document:

IN THE DISTRICT COURT

IN AND FOR THE COUNTY OF LARIMER

AND STATE OF COLORADO

Division I

Civil Action No. 20395

ANNE RASMUSSEN,	)	
	)	
Plaintiff,	)	
	)	
vs.	)	JUDGMENT
	)	
PAULA GRAHAM and ROGER GRAHAM,	)	
	)	
Defendants.	)	

---

changed "willful and wanton" to "willful or wanton," by crossing out "and" and writing in "or." Some of the jurors were afraid that "wanton" suggested sexual abandon, and were therefore unwilling to apply that word to Paula's conduct. By changing "and" to "or," these jurors were satisfied that they had not said that Paula had been "wanton."

Unfortunately, the jury had been discharged, and could not be reassembled. The statute required a finding of both willful *and* wanton behavior, before a "guest" could recover against her host. Because the jury had not found that both behaviors were present, their finding on this issue could not be used to support liability. If the jury's finding of "payment" could not be affirmed, the "willful and wanton" issue would have to be entirely retried by a new jury.

This action came for trial before the Court and a jury, the Honorable John Shannon presiding, and the issues having been duly tried and the jury having duly rendered its verdict,

It is Ordered and Adjudged that the plaintiff Anne Rasmussen recover of the defendant Paula Graham the sum of $97,000.00, with interest thereon at the rate of six percent per annum as provided by law, and her costs of action.

Based upon an Order of the Court, it is further Ordered and Adjudged that the plaintiff Anne Rasmussen take nothing of the defendant Roger Graham, that the case against Roger Graham be dismissed, and that Roger Graham recover of plaintiff Anne Rasmussen his costs of action, with interest thereon at the rate of six percent per annum as provided by law.

Dated at Fort Collins, Colorado, this 14th day of June, 1995.

[Signed] Roger Finger
Clerk of the Court

This document was then filed in a large book referred to as the judgment docket. Copies were filed, in alphabetical order, under Paula's name and Anne's name, as both now had judgments against them.

The judgment is the operative document, sought as the end result of the litigation. As long as an effective judgment is on file, the person in whose favor the judgment was rendered (the judgment creditor) can use the coercive power of the state to force payment by the person against whom the judgment runs (the judgment debtor). The judgment debtor generally cannot be imprisoned for nonpayment of the judgment, but the sheriff may seize and sell as much of the judgment debtor's property as is necessary to satisfy the judgment. Furthermore, bank accounts of the judgment debtor can be seized, and the debtor's employer can be ordered to pay a certain proportion of the debtor's wages, as they come due, directly to the sheriff for the benefit of the judgment creditor. To avoid the imposition of such onerous means of collection, a judgment debtor who is able to pay the amount of the judgment usually will do so.

b. Post-Verdict Motions

i. Motion for judgment notwithstanding the verdict (Judgment n.o.v.) (Fed. R. Civ. P. 51(B))

This motion, also known as a post-trial motion for judgment as a matter of law, asks the court to order judgment for one litigant despite a jury verdict in favor of the other. The party making such a motion contends that a directed verdict should have been granted before the case was submitted to the jury. Only a party who previously moved for a directed verdict can move for judgment notwithstanding the verdict. The provisions for a motion for judgment n.o.v. make it possible for the judge to defer ruling on the propriety of a directed verdict.

It is often advantageous for the court to deny a motion for a directed verdict even when the court feels that a directed verdict is warranted, because a judge's ruling ordering a directed verdict is appealable, but a jury's verdict is not. If the court allows the case to go to the jury, the jury may return a verdict in favor of the party the court believes is entitled to a directed verdict. The judgment in that party's favor will rest on a firmer foundation if it is based on a verdict rather than on the court's own determination. If the court were to grant the motion for a directed verdict, the losing party could appeal that ruling. The appellate court might disagree with the trial court on the propriety of the directed verdict and reverse the judgment. In that case a new trial would be necessary and efforts expended in the earlier one would be wasted.

If the motion for directed verdict is denied and the jury returns a verdict against the party the court felt was entitled to a directed verdict, the court can still order judgment in that party's favor by granting a motion for judgment n.o.v. That ruling can be appealed, of course, but if the appellate court disagrees with the trial judge a new trial will not be necessary. The appellate court can simply order that the jury's verdict be reinstated and judgment entered in accordance with it.

ii. Motion for new trial

Successful motions to dismiss, motions for summary judgments, and motions for judgments n.o.v. all result in a final judgment in favor of the moving party. A successful motion for new trial, however, merely means that the parties may litigate the case again. The party against whom the new trial was granted has a chance to win again. New trials are granted generally in two situations. First, where some error or unforeseen occurrence happens during the course of the trial and the judge believes that the jury could not for that reason reach a fair verdict. Second, where the judge feels that the evidence was very strongly against the decision reached by the jury. This could happen when the party who prevailed with the jury presented "substantial evidence" on every necessary point, but the judge felt that the evidence was not very convincing.

Wilton moved for a new trial on the theory that the court's submission of the payment issue to the jury was in error. This would not support a motion for judgment n.o.v., because even if the "payment" issue were kept from the jury, that would only have precluded recovery in Anne's first claim for relief. She would still be entitled to get to the jury on her third claim for relief, the "willful and wanton" issue. If the court were mistaken on the "payment" issue, the jury's verdict on the "willful and wanton" issue would become important, and retrial on that issue would be necessary because of the jury's failure to answer the statutory question.

Wilton submitted a fairly detailed memorandum supporting his motion for new trial. Hart countered, also with a substantial memorandum. After oral argument, Judge Shannon ruled that there was sufficient evidence to support a finding of payment, and therefore he had not erred in submitting that issue to the jury. The motion was denied.

D. THE APPEAL

From the very beginning of the litigation Wilton had contended that on the facts of this case, there was not sufficient evidence of payment to permit that issue to be given to the jury, that there had been no payment as a "matter of law." Ultimately the trial judge ruled against this contention. Wilton felt quite strongly that Judge Shannon was wrong on the payment issue, and on his advice Safeco authorized an appeal.

The appellate process is commenced by the filing of a notice of appeal. This is simply a brief formal statement, indicating the party who is appealing, and the judgment or order from which he is appealing. In this case, the notice of appeal was as follows:

IN THE DISTRICT COURT

IN AND FOR THE COUNTY OF LARIMER

AND STATE OF COLORADO

Division I

Civil Action No. 20395

ANNE RASMUSSEN,	)	
	)	
Plaintiff,	)	
	)	
vs.	)	NOTICE OF APPEAL
	)	
PAULA GRAHAM and ROGER GRAHAM,	)	
	)	
Defendants.	)	

Defendant Paula Graham, by her attorney Alfred Wilton, hereby files this notice of appeal from the Court's denial of defendant's motion for New Trial.

June 27, 1995   [Signed] Alfred Wilton
                                            Attorney for Defendant
                                            [Address and Telephone
                                            Omitted]

This document was submitted to the clerk of the court, with a copy to Hart.

At the same time, Wilton moved that execution of the judgment be stayed, pending the appeal. You will remember that a judgment for $97,000 had been entered against Paula. Wilton and Paula were both anxious that payment of this judgment be put off until it was clear whether or not the judgment was proper. If execution were not stayed, then Anne could force payment of the full amount of the judgment. If Anne collected and spent the money, and then the judgment was reversed on appeal, how could Paula (or Safeco) recover the money paid to Anne under the erroneous judgment?

On the other hand, if execution of a judgment could be stayed merely by filing an appeal, every losing defendant would be tempted to file an appeal, just to put off the moment of having to pay. During this time, assets which the prevailing plaintiff should have been able to use for the satisfaction of her judgment may be consumed by the losing party, leaving nothing to satisfy the judgment when it was ultimately affirmed on appeal.

These conflicting interests are usually resolved as follows: once a plaintiff has obtained a judgment, it is presumed that she is entitled to have it paid, whether or not defendant appeals. If defendant wishes to delay execution pending appeal, she must post a bond guaranteeing payment of the judgment (with interest) should the judgment be affirmed. If such a bond is posted, plaintiff will lose the benefit of having the money immediately, but she will be guaranteed prompt and complete satisfaction of her judgment if she wins on appeal.

The bond guaranteeing payment of the judgment is referred to as a "supersedeas bond." Safeco filed such a bond, and the judge ordered a stay of execution. The Clerk, in turn, made a notation on the judgment form in the judgment docket, showing that execution of the judgment had been stayed.

At least as a theoretical matter, no facts are determined at the appellate level. All factual information concerning the case must come from the trial court. This information is contained in the record and the transcript. The record consists of the formal pleadings in the case, certain motions, and such other formal documents from the trial court proceeding as either party wishes to have included. The appellate court also considers those parts of the court reporter's transcript that either party considers appropriate. The process of instructing the clerk of the trial court about which documents to include is referred to as designating the record on appeal.

Within a certain period of time after the notice of appeal and designation of the record, the appellant must file a brief. The brief serves three main functions:

1. In its "statement of the case," it summarizes and presents the case to the appellate court. The statement of the case must do no more than present information already in the record, but the manner in which it does this is very important to the way in which the appellate court will approach the case.

2. The main function of the brief is the presentation of the attorney's argument.

3. The brief also sets out the relief the appellant seeks from the appellate court.

Appellate courts usually have between three and nine judges deciding each case. The parties must send a sufficient number of briefs to the clerk of the court, so that a copy of each brief can be distributed to each judge who will be participating in the case.

After the Appellant's Opening Brief, the Appellee's Brief, and the Appellant's reply brief have all been filed, the case is set for oral argument. Most appellate courts allow each side 20 or 30 minutes for oral argument. The appellant presents arguments first, and if desired may reserve a few minutes of her allotted time for rebuttal following the appellee's arguments. During the course of oral arguments, the judges will frequently interrupt to ask questions of the attorney. This is extremely valuable to the attorney, as it shows her what concerns the judges have about the case and provides her with an opportunity to respond to those concerns. Indeed, most appellate attorneys would be concerned if they were allowed to complete their prepared oral argument, as this would suggest that the judges were not interested in their position.

Once every few days or once a week the members of the court will meet for a brief conference on the cases that have been argued since the last conference. There will be a discussion of the case, followed by a preliminary vote. One of the members of the preliminary majority will be assigned the task of writing the opinion for the case.[20]

---

[20] If the Chief Justice is in the preliminary majority, she will assign the case. If the Chief Justice is not in the majority, the senior justice in the majority (in terms of years on the Court) will assign the case.

When the late Chief Justice Warren Burger was first appointed to the United States Supreme Court in 1973, he took it upon himself to assign cases even when he was not voting with the majority. The other justices quickly dissuaded him from this practice. Can you see why there would be a problem with having a justice (even the Chief Justice) decide which justice should write the majority opinion when the assigning justice is opposed to the position of the majority?

Within a few weeks of the conference, the assigned justice will prepare an opinion in which she sets forth her view of the case and the arguments in favor of the majority's position. The draft is circulated to each of the members of the court. If a justice agrees with the opinion, she will simply sign on. She might also agree with the basic thrust but disagree with portions of the opinion; in that case, she will ask the writer to change those portions. If the writer does, she will then join the opinion. If the writer does not, she may join the parts of the opinion that she agrees with, or refuse to join the opinion and write her own opinion; because it agrees with the outcome, such an opinion would be referred to as a "separate concurring opinion." If a justice disagrees with the outcome of the initial opinion, she will usually write her own "dissenting opinion" or join a dissenting opinion written by one of the other justices.

If an opinion is joined by a majority of the justices, it then becomes an official expression of the court's position and is referred to as "the opinion of the court." As such, it will be controlling precedent for all future cases in the state, unless and until it is overruled. If an opinion is not joined by a majority of the justices of the court, it is nothing more than an expression of the personal position of the justice who wrote the opinion and the justices who indicated their agreement with her. Therefore, the person who writes the draft opinion is usually interested in accommodating enough of the other justices to form a majority while still remaining true to her beliefs regarding the case. Occasionally one of the other opinions, either concurring or dissenting, will be able to pick up a majority. In this case, the justice who wrote the original draft will usually stick with her opinion, which will then be a either a separate concurring opinion or a dissenting opinion.

It is essential to this process that no opinion be released to the public until every justice has had an opportunity to join or respond to each of the opinions circulating in the case and each of the writers has had an opportunity to respond to each of the other justices' comments. When none of the justices has anything further to write, the opinions are released. The Court's opinion will come first, followed by separate concurring opinions, which are then followed by dissenting opinions. If there are two concurring opinions or two dissenting opinions, the opinion joined by the chief justice or the most senior justice will be placed ahead of the other opinion.

At times the justices are sufficiently divided in their views that no opinion can capture a majority. In this situation, there will be no opinion of the court. If there is a majority in favor of affirming, the judgment appealed will be affirmed; if there is a majority in favor of reversing, the judgment will be reversed. In either event, there will be no official explanation of the court's position. The justices will write or join separate opinions explaining and arguing for their respective positions.

Where there is no majority opinion, the opinion gathering the most votes will be referred to as the "plurality opinion;" the plurality opinion will come first in order (the position occupied by the majority opinion, when there is one) and will announce the outcome of the case (which is referred to as the court's "decision" of the case). If there is a tie among potential plurality opinions (e.g., three justices join one opinion, three join another, and the remaining justice or justices write individual opinions), the opinion joined by the chief justice will be treated as the plurality; it will be printed in the first position and will announce the court's decision. If the chief justice joins neither of the two opinions, the opinion which has been joined by the most senior justice will be published first. (This position is of some importance, because plurality opinions look so much like majority opinions that they are frequently treated as such by the profession, even though (in theory) they should not be.)

Most states now have two levels of appellate courts: an intermediate level (frequently referred to as the "District Court of Appeals" or "Circuit Court of Appeals") and a highest level, usually (but not always) referred to as "the Supreme Court."[21] After the judgment in the trial court, either party is automatically entitled to appeal to the intermediate court simply by filing a timely notice of appeal.

The party who loses in the intermediate appellate court does not have automatic access to the highest court. Usually the highest court will only hear those cases which it considers to be of importance to the entire system. The United States Supreme Court provides the most extreme example. Because of the large amount of time involved in deciding each case, the Supreme Court can hear argument and issue opinions in only about 150 cases a year. Yet there are tens of thousands of cases decided by the United States Circuit Courts of Appeals, and at least that many capable of being appealed to the United States Supreme Court from state appellate courts. So when the Court decides which cases to hear each year, it will choose cases so that each of the 150 or so opinions it can issue each year will have the maximum effect in the many important areas the Court must supervise, including constitutional rights, interpretation of federal statutes, supervision of federal court procedure, and supervision of federal administrative practices. The situation is similar, though less extreme, in most state court systems.

If the party who lost in the intermediate appellate court wishes Supreme Court review, she must convince the Supreme Court that the issues raised by this case need to be addressed on a nationwide or statewide basis; of course, if the

---

[21] Variations among the states can be confusing. In New York, for example, the trial court of general jurisdiction is the "Supreme Court;" the intermediate appellate court is "The Supreme Court, Appellate Division," and the highest appellate court is "The Court of Appeals." A small number of other states also refer to their highest appellate courts as "The Court of Appeals."

attorney can convince the court that a serious error or serious injustice occurred in the intermediate appellate court, that will only help.

When a party wishes to have Supreme Court review, she must petition the Supreme Court to have her case heard. In the federal courts and in most state courts, she will file a "Petition for a Writ of Certiorari." In English, this is a petition requesting the Supreme Court to issue an order to the intermediate court, instructing that court to certify the record in the case and transfer that record to the Supreme Court. Her petition will be supported by a brief. The other party will then have a period of time in which to file a brief in opposition to the petition; having prevailed in the intermediate court, she of course would prefer no further appellate review. The petitioner will then have an opportunity for a reply to the brief in opposition. In due course, the Supreme Court will issue an order either granting or denying the petition. Of course, granting a Petition for Certiorari does not reverse the lower court, it only accepts jurisdiction over the appeal.

In the United States Supreme Court, Certiorari Petitions have an unusual aspect; while the Court generally acts only by majority, a petition for certiorari will be granted if four of the nine justices vote for it. The Supreme Court seldom, if ever, issues opinions when it grants certiorari. Occasionally (but very seldom) a justice will write a dissenting opinion when the Court denies certiorari in a case which she considers to be particularly cert-worthy.

After the judgment in *Rasmussen v. Graham*, the parties continued their guest statute battle in the Colorado appellate courts. The jury's change of the jury form meant that plaintiff did not have a usable finding of "willful and wanton disregard" to support her judgment. Thus, her judgment depended upon the jury's determination that there was payment for the transportation. If Wilton could get that determination reversed, plaintiff's judgment would be vacated and a new trial would be granted.

Throughout the case, Wilton had been frustrated by the trial court's treatment of the "payment" issue. As Wilton read the Colorado Supreme Court cases, an agreement to share expenses on a social trip was by definition *not* payment within the statute. While there might have been one recent Colorado Court of Appeals opinion which created a very small inroad on that principle (*Burgoyne*, discussed page 50, *supra*), that was not a Supreme Court opinion, and the plaintiff in that case was in the car *only* for the defendant's benefit. In Wilton's view, the Supreme Court opinions had spoken clearly, and he was frustrated that Hart had been able (in Wilton's opinion) to convince Judge Shannon to ignore or misread those opinions.

The clearest and most frequently cited of the Colorado Supreme Court opinions was *Mears v. Kovacic*.

Mears and Kovacic were both residents of Grand Junction and had been close friends for some fifteen years, such close friends that on a snowy winter day

Mears, who had no car, asked Kovacic to drive him to Denver. The reason for this urgent request was that Mears had just learned that his wife, who was in Denver, was sick and accordingly he desired to see her at once and hoped to bring her back to Grand Junction. In connection with his request, Mears volunteered to pay Kovacic's expenses "if he would take me to Denver to get my wife and bring her back." When asked what expenses he had in mind, Mears replied: "All incidental expenses to the trip such as gasoline, oil, food, lodging." Although it was clearly established that Kovacic himself had no reason to go to Denver, he nevertheless agreed to aid Mears, and within one hour the two were headed toward Denver in Kovacic's automobile and with Kovacic at the wheel.

Before leaving Grand Junction Mears "borrowed a set of chains because Kovacic did not have any." Mears then bought and paid for a tank of gas in Grand Junction. A stop was made in Glenwood Springs, where Mears bought and paid for coffee. At Dillon, Mears bought sandwiches for the two of them and also paid to have the chains put on the car. A short time later, with Mears half asleep and "leaning back on the seat," Mears testified that he felt the "car give a little, just slip a little bit and then it caught on the shoulder of the road and we went over ... it happened fairly fast, and we were going a little fast ... around 35 miles per hour."

On cross examination Mears admitted that he hoped Kovacic would drive him to Denver because "he was a good friend." He then conceded that he did not contemplate payment to Kovacic of any sum for the depreciation of his car, was only going to pay him for "gas and oil and other expenses" and agreed that Kovacic was "not going to get any money out of this thing."

The Colorado Supreme Court forcefully rejected Mears' suggestion that payment for expenses could constitute "payment" under the guest statute. The court quoted with approval from a number of opinions from other states, in which agreements to share expenses had been held not to constitute "payment":

> In *Riggs v. Roberts*, the Supreme Court of Idaho stated that "[t]he courts have quite uniformly held that merely paying for gas and oil or sharing the payment for gas and oil is not of itself and alone sufficient to establish passenger status," passenger status being therein defined as "one riding for compensation."

> In *Bedenbender v. Walls*, the Supreme Court of Kansas, which state has a guest statute virtually identical to that of Colorado, declared the following:

> ....

> The facts already have been related and will not be repeated. They clearly show a situation of common everyday experience to everyone, that of reciprocal hospitality and social courtesy between friends when the undertaking is for the mutual social pleasure of the parties concerned. There was no relationship of mutual benefit between or among them other

than of a social nature. The payment of certain traveling expenses by plaintiff husband amounted to nothing more than the exchange of social amenities and did not transform plaintiffs' status into that of passengers "for pay," when, without such exchange, they would be guests, and consequently was not "payment for such transportation" within the meaning of the statute. To hold otherwise would compel every host to dilute his hospitality and season it with the flavor of a bargain. The record presented supports only the conclusion that the sole purpose of the trip was the joint pleasure of the parties. Friendship and sociability were the basis of plaintiffs being in the car. In fact, we have no doubt but that at the time in question the parties would have resented any suggestion that their relationship was anything other than social and for mutual pleasure. One occupying the status of a guest should not be permitted to accept a gratuity under mental reservation, and, by a trifling reciprocity, convert it into a binding agreement having legal consequences.

The court affirmed the trial court's refusal to send the payment issue to the jury. (other leading cases on the issue are discussed above; see pages 49-50, *supra*.)

So Wilton approached the appeal with some confidence. He had based his advice against settlement, as well as his plan for trial of the case, on the belief that the appellate courts would not permit "payment" to be found in such an overwhelmingly social context, at least not without a much more clearly defined benefit sought by and conferred upon the defendant. Wilton recognized that his position was unsympathetic, but had confidence that sympathy would yield to what he saw as clear and simple logic.

QUESTION

After reading the excerpt from *Mears v. Kovacic* set out above, do you disagree with Wilton's reading of Colorado law? In his position, what advice would you have given Safeco regarding settlement at the outset of the case?

1. THE RULING OF THE COLORADO COURT OF APPEALS

Wilton appealed the trial court's denial of his pre-verdict and post-verdict motions for judgment as a matter of law (directed verdict motion and motion for judgment notwithstanding the verdict, respectively) to the Colorado Court of Appeals. The parties submitted their briefs, and ultimately had oral argument on the payment issue. Within a fairly brief period of time, the Court of Appeals decided the case:

RASMUSSEN v. GRAHAM

Colorado Court of Appeals

SMITH, JUDGE:

Defendants appeal from a judgment entered on a jury verdict awarding plaintiff damages for injuries received in an automobile accident. Although defendants have asserted numerous errors, it is only necessary for us to consider the application of the guest statute. We reverse.

As grounds for recovery, plaintiffs' complaint asserted both simple negligence and conduct consisting of a willful and wanton disregard for the rights, safety and well-being of plaintiff. Defendants asserted the guest statute as an affirmative defense. Although defendants moved for a ruling as a matter of law that plaintiff was a guest under the guest statute, the court submitted instructions to the jury on simple negligence and on willful and wanton conduct. The jury was instructed that if it found that plaintiff was a guest it had to apply the willful and wanton standard. However, it was instructed that if it found plaintiff was not a guest, it could apply the simple negligence standard.

The pertinent evidence at trial was not in dispute and was consistent in establishing that plaintiff and defendant had taken skiing trips together from Fort Collins to Steamboat Springs, and that plaintiff customarily paid one-half of the gas. On the trip in issue in this case, plaintiff traveled in defendant's car from Fort Collins to Steamboat Springs where she was the guest of defendant and her parents at their trailer in Steamboat Springs. On the day of the accident, plaintiff was a passenger in defendant's car as they were returning from a trip from Steamboat Springs to Craig. Plaintiff was not required to pay expenses while staying at defendant's parents' trailer and was in every way treated as a guest on the trip. The side trip between Steamboat Springs and Craig was for the sole purpose of defendant's obtaining a key to the trailer house and was conducted outside the arrangement concerning gasoline for the trip between Fort Collins and Steamboat Springs. There was undisputed evidence that on excursions around town plaintiff did not pay for gas, and the testimony established that defendant's father had filled the tank on the morning of the accident.

To remove plaintiff from guest status, any payment made must be a special tangible benefit, accruing to defendant as a motivating influence for furnishing transportation to plaintiff. *Klatka v. Barker*. It is evident from the present facts that plaintiff was invited on the trip because her friend desired her companionship. This is true concerning the trip from Fort Collins to Steamboat Springs, and is even more true of the side trip from Steamboat Springs to Craig. There was no evidence to support a decision by the jury that plaintiff was not a guest. When there is no serious dispute as to the facts, the question of the party's status as a guest is one of law. We hold that, as a matter of law, plaintiff was a guest under the terms of the guest statute, and the trial court should have so ruled.

It was thus error from the trial court to have submitted for the jury's determination the question of whether plaintiff was a guest. The jury should have been instructed as a matter of law that plaintiff was a guest and no instruction permitting a verdict on simple negligence should have been given. Hence, the judgment rendered on that verdict cannot be upheld on review. We reverse the judgment and remand the cause for a new trial.

SILVERSTEIN, C.J., and PIERCE, J., concurring.

Hart, of course, was unhappy with this result, and he petitioned the Colorado Supreme Court for a writ of certiorari. Apparently sensing that the payment issue required authoritative clarification, the Colorado Supreme Court granted Hart's petition for certiorari. After briefs and oral argument, the Court issued the following, final opinion in this case:

2. THE RULING OF THE COLORADO SUPREME COURT

RASMUSSEN v. GRAHAM

Colorado Supreme Court

PRINGLE, CHIEF JUSTICE:

In this proceeding, certiorari was granted to review the decision of the Court of Appeals. The case arises out of an automobile accident wherein the defendant-respondent was the driver and plaintiff-petitioner was her passenger. The issue for review involves the application of the "guest" statute. The trial court submitted to the jury in the form of a special interrogatory the issue of whether petitioner was respondent's guest. The jury found that the host-guest relationship did not exist and returned a verdict for petitioner. The Court of Appeals held that, as a matter of law, petitioner was a guest within the meaning of the statute and that it was reversible error to have submitted the issue to the jury.

Petitioner contends that the Court of Appeals erred in holding that the petitioner was a guest as a matter of law. The evidence shows that the petitioner and respondent had been friends for some time prior to the accident. The girls had taken a number of trips together where petitioner had been respondent's passenger and was expected to and did pay her share of the cost of the gasoline used. In December 1993 respondent invited petitioner to go with her to Steamboat Springs for a skiing holiday. The girls decided that respondent would purchase the gasoline for the trip to Steamboat Springs and petitioner would pay for the gasoline on the way back. Respondent purchased the gasoline, and they went to Steamboat Springs. There the girls stayed with respondent's parents in their trailer. On the day of the accident, respondent's father had occasion to use his daughter's car, and he filled it with gasoline. Because of electrical problems in the trailer, the girls were told they could not stay in the trailer after the parents' departure. Thus, respondent decided to go to Craig to have a duplicate key made for the trailer so she and the petitioner would be able to stay in the trailer without the parents' knowledge. The girls went to Craig and on the return trip the collision occurred, resulting in petitioner's injuries.

We begin by pointing out that it is not the passenger who must establish that he *was not* a guest, but rather it is the person who is relying on the "guest" statute who has the burden of establishing that the passenger *was* a guest. The general rule is that a person is not a guest if he confers a benefit upon the owner or operator of a car which is sufficiently real, tangible and substantial and is an inducing cause for furnishing the transportation. *Klatka v. Barker*. Sharing expenses of an automobile trip is an incident of a relationship between passenger and driver which may negate the guest-host relationship required under the "guest" statute. [Here the Court cited one of its car pool cases, which had arisen in a work context.]

Here there was evidence from which the jury could find that such a sharing expense situation existed, that it was a real, tangible and substantial benefit to the driver, that an inducing cause to the driver to take this passenger was her agreement to share the expenses, and that it was of mutual benefit to both parties. This is in contra-distinction to *Mears v. Kovacic*, where the arrangement was made as a favor to the passenger and for his sole benefit. It is, of course, not necessary that the payment be the only cause or even the primary inducement for the carrying of the passenger to exempt the relationship from one of guest and host.

There was sufficient evidence here to, at least, go to the jury on the question of whether the guest-host relationship existed here. Under such circumstances, an appellate court may not substitute its judgment for that of the jury.

The judgment of the Court of Appeals is reversed and the case is remanded to the Court of Appeals for further disposition not inconsistent with this opinion.

GROVES, JUSTICE and ERICKSON, JUSTICE (concurring in the result):

In our view, the effect of this opinion is to overrule *Mears v. Kovacic*, and it should be overruled.

QUESTIONS

1. Is this majority opinion consistent with the earlier cases? If not, what content does this opinion give to the term "guest, without payment"? Should the court have squarely overruled its earlier opinion? If so, why? If not, why not?

2. Should Wilton have anticipated the possibility of this outcome? Do you believe his advice to Safeco was prudent? If not, what led him astray? Did he misread the cases? Did he have too much confidence that they would be applied exactly as they were written?

3. Would we have a better system if cases and statutes were applied as strictly as Wilton had anticipated? Is it possible to have a system in which cases and statutes are applied as strictly as Wilton had anticipated? If it is, would you rather live under that system, or under our own?